How to *Fight* for Your
MARRIAGE
without Fighting with One Another
(Using a 2-Step Process)

Dr. Raymond Force

Printed in the United States of America

ISBN 978-163443628-1

Published by Hitting Home
www.HittingHomeMinistry.com

Hitting Home
P.O. Box 1452
Anthony, FL 32617

To my parents.
Thank you for your unbiased support.

In Christ "are hid
all the treasures of
wisdom and knowledge."

CONTENTS

How to Use
this Book in a
Bible Study Setting

This book has been designed for you to use in a group study as well as on an individual basis. Here are a few helpful hints if you choose to lead a Bible study group using this resource:

1. Assign a chapter or two at a time for the members of the group to read. Depending on the length of the chapter, you may have to adjust the amount of chapters assigned. Some of our chapters are much longer than others. Therefore, at times, you may want to assign half of a chapter or so.

2. When the group meets back together, the leader may want to start by relaying what meant the most to him or her. They may even want to read a specific section to the group, so as to remind the group of the chapter's content.

3. After the leader relays his or her thoughts, he or she may want to open the floor for a brief time of discussion, as to what spoke the most to the individual members of the group. Keep in mind, since you are dealing with marriage, a few group members may want to monopolize the study time with specific details of their own marriage. A leader may need to kindly set boundaries before the study begins so as to avoid this scenario, as it will prove to be unprofitable for all involved. In such cases, we would recommend encouraging the said persons to find Christian-based counseling, to better facilitate their needs.

4. We have placed thought provoking questions at the end of every chapter. It is recommended that you ask and answer those at every setting.

5. You will notice that we have placed scriptures by some of the questions. We would recommend that you read these scriptures as you discuss your answers.

6. We also have an audio series that may aid the members of the group to better understand the content of the book. This series may be ordered at www.Shop. HittingHomeMinistry.com. This audio series is in CD or MP3 format.

Chapter 1

THE WHY BEHIND THE WHAT

Marriage is for God

During our marriage conferences, I have found it vital to begin by talking about the why behind the what. I choose this as an opening topic because it is the why that determines how you do the what. That is, it is the why that dictates your level of commitment and intensity toward the what.

That being said, why is it so important to deal with the subject of marriage? Why further your knowledge on the subject? First and foremost, God's glory is at stake.

Typically, when we think of having a marriage conference or seminar, we envision people packing into a room or an auditorium and learning how to have happier marriages. The only problem is that there is much more at stake than our own happiness.

I often say that husbands and wives are two very different looking pieces of the same two-piece puzzle. When they fit together in love and unity, they make a beautiful picture of the glory of God and especially

Christ's love for the church. When those two pieces fail to come together, the picture that others should be seeing is tragically obscured.

If you claim to be a Christ-follower, others are watching you, especially your children. If you do not have the hot and harmonious relationship with your spouse that God would have you to enjoy, onlookers are either consciously or subconsciously asking themselves, "Is that all that God can do in a Christian home?"

Upon broaching this subject, some are prone to ask, "Doesn't God want me to be happy?" Though I am inclined to answer in the positive, I would be amiss if I fail to point out the following:

> Those in life that make it their primary goal to be happy seldom ever reach that goal. Those that find true and long-lasting happiness make it their main objective to make God happy.

This was the essence of Christ's teachings in Matthew 16:25. In Matthew's gospel, Christ taught:

> *"For whosoever will save his life shall lose it: and whosoever will lose his life for my sake shall find it."*
> *(Matthew 16:25)*

Adrian Rogers said it like this:

> "Happiness is something you stumble over on your way to serving Jesus. When you are serving the Lord Jesus Christ, happiness is the by-product of righteousness."[1]

I have found it to be vital for couples to make God's goal their goal in the marital relationship. Though this may seem to be a trivial matter to some, here are a few reasons as to its importance:

1. If God instituted marriage, then why would His main concern not be ours? (Isaiah 43:21, Isaiah 43:7, and Isaiah 44:23)

If we are going to put our minds on the subject of marriage, then should we not be thinking about what He deems to be of utmost importance, His glory? (I Corinthians 10:31) Is it not a disservice to push aside His glory to simply focus on the happiness of man?

It is my belief that God's glory is the most missing element in even our Christian-based marriage material today. That is, marriage is not about finding happiness as much as it is about displaying God's power and love through the medium of marriage. Any other approach, no matter how Christian it appears to be, is mere humanism with a veneer of Christianity.

2. Husbands and wives that make it their supreme goal to be happy in a marriage experience a diminished level of strength and endurance during the more stressful times.

During days of emotional darkness, many husbands and wives fail to see the light of happiness at the end of the tunnel. It is at this point that many become disillusioned and discouraged about their marriage. Consequently, they tend to lack the emotional and spiritual stamina it takes to keep moving in a positive direction.

The scriptures teach in Proverbs 29:18 that "where there is no vision, the people perish." This principle is applicable to marriage, in that when spouses fail to see an end in sight of their pain and misery, the marriage typically starts the dying process and their strength to persevere begins to wane.

Be that as it may, what if spouses in a troubled marriage understand that the purpose for marriage is not so much finding happiness, but glorifying God? Now the paradigm is entirely different, in that they now have a goal that can be reached on a daily basis despite the selfish behavior of the other. The scenario has changed. Now, no matter how the other person in the marriage behaves, each participant can consistently reach their goal of bringing glory to God.

Your spouse may be able to control a number of things in your life, but they are unable to control your obedience to God. Thus, they are unable to keep you from obtaining spiritual joy by glorifying the Lord through your thoughts, actions, and deeds. (Psalm 1:1-2 and Luke 11:28)

Many spouses feel out of control when it comes to their marriage. They almost feel that the other person holds their happiness as a hostage because they persist in a pattern of sin and selfishness. Spouses in such a case will do well to recognize that only God should hold that much power over their emotions, and the real obstacle to emotional freedom is never anyone but themselves.

Figuratively speaking, the door to unhappiness and discontentment always opens from the inside, even in a troubled marriage.

3. God's people have something to prove.

In much of the book of Deuteronomy, the Lord commands His people what to do once they enter into the land of Canaan. In Deuteronomy 4, however, God does not teach His people what to do, as much as why they should submit to His ways. Below is a snippet from Deuteronomy 4:5-8:

> *"Behold, I have taught you statutes and judgments, even as the LORD my God commanded me, that ye should do so in the land whither ye go to possess it. Keep therefore and do them; for this is your wisdom and your understanding in the sight of the nations, which shall hear all these statutes, and say, Surely this great nation is a wise and understanding people. For what nation is there so great, who hath God so nigh unto them, as the LORD our God is in all things that we call upon him for? And what nation is there so great, that hath statutes and judgments so righteous as all this law, which I set before you this day?"*

In short, God knew that other nations that did not know Him were going to observe the Israelites once they settled in the land of Canaan. As they beheld their works,

He wanted them to come to one primary conclusion: What a great God is the God of the Israelites!

Though others may disagree with our theology and our life choices as they relate to scripture, they should not be able to argue with the results of serving the Lord.

Proverbs 13:15 says that "the way of transgressors is hard," yet Proverbs 3:17 states that biblical wisdom leads us into "ways of pleasantness." In a day when some say that the divorce rate is as high as fifty percent, God's people have a unique opportunity to display that His ways yield better results.

I believe it was Amy Carmichael who said that bright lights were not made for sunny rooms, but for dark places. That being the case, God's people are in a great position to shine the results of His ways in this very dark world in which we live. We are in a wonderful position to lead others to have to say, "What a great God is the God of the church!"

4. If a person only marries to find happiness, then they are chasing a mirage.

Marriage has the best sales yet, with the worst advertising of any product on the market. As a result, it still amazes me how many singles look to a relationship with the opposite gender or marriage itself as a major source for happiness.

Though marriage is a marvelous institution, it must be noted that happy singles make happy married people. If a person is unhappy or unfulfilled before marriage, unless something changes within, they will also be unhappy after they make their covenant.

Here is one of the many ways that I describe what makes a great marriage:

> A great marriage is when two full-grown adults wake up with their cup of happiness and fulfillment full to overflowing. What spills out of that cup is what should land on the other person.

Do you wake up happy despite the behavior of your spouse? Or, has it been your custom to go through the day thinking that if your spouse would make the right changes, then you could see yourself being happy?

If you are waiting for your spouse to change before feeling happy and content, then you are chasing a mirage. Quite simply, you are investing in a stock that will always yield few returns, in that your spouse is too small to be your sole source of emotional and spiritual sustenance. In fact, I often teach that looking to your spouse for happiness and fulfillment can be likened to trying to fill a 55 gallon barrel with a thimble full of water. Your spouse is simply too small in comparison with God.

The promises of God concerning your own happiness and contentment never hinge upon your spouse's obedience or disobedience to God. In fact, the promises of God concerning happiness and joy only rely upon the faithfulness of a loving God. Any other approach will cause your emotional state to be like a yo-yo on the string of your spouse's inconsistencies, and you will be prone to be up one day and down the next.

When couples enter into marriage looking for happiness, they end up becoming two ticks with no dog. That is, they suck the life right out of each other, and it is not too long before they are looking elsewhere for fulfillment.

Psalm 16:11 tells us that in God's presence there is "fullness of joy." The usage of the word "fullness" teaches us that there is no room for improvement upon the joy that God supplies.

Marriage, on the other hand, is the exact opposite, in that, after the wedding day, we quickly see areas in ourselves, the other person, and in the relationship that are often lacking.

Notwithstanding, lest some feel that I have some type of monastic or stoic attitude toward marriage, I would like to point out that I believe that marriage should be a joyful experience.

Proverbs 5:19 tells us that the husband is to always be ravished with the love of his wife. According to Webster's dictionary from 1828, the word ravished means to delight to ecstasy. The word ecstasy means to be carried away with extreme delight or joy. Therefore, we can conclude that marriage is to be an emotionally fulfilling relationship, but only after Christ has become what your spouse can never be; your all in all. (Ephesians 1:23)

I deem marriage to be the icing on top of the cake. That is, matrimony is a fringe benefit to what the Lord has already done in our lives. Unfortunately, some men and women have little or no cake upon which that icing can rest. In such cases, their mates often grow weary in their attempts at blessing them, as, deep down, they know they can never take the place of God in their lives.

The Church must have
Something Worth Reproducing

The church's responsibility is not merely to see lost people come to Christ. It is also to reproduce in others what God has already done in them. (Matthew 28:19-20)

That said, it should be understood that when we invite people to church, or to be a part of the family of God, we are asking them to come and be like us. Even if that is not our intent, it is still inferred. Hence, it is vital for believers to ask themselves a few heart-searching questions as they endeavor to reach people for Christ:

Question #1: Do we have a right to ask people to come and be like us if our homes are not moving toward a Biblical standard?

Question #2: Do we have something worth reproducing in the lives of others if we are not, at the very least, desiring God's best for our homes.

The Church is to Uphold God's Truth

I Timothy 3:15 tells us that the church is "the pillar and the ground of the truth." A pillar serves the purpose of holding up a structure. Without pillars, many buildings would fall down flat.

According to I Timothy 3, the church is God's pillar to hold up the truth concerning His Word and His ways. Hence, if His church fails to bring His ways to light, what other people group will bear His torch?

Concerning the home, it is the church's responsibility to exalt God's truth about marriage, parenting, and issues pertaining to the family. If the church fails to shine this light, outside of conscience and the scriptures, no other source exists.

The True Test of Your Christianity is How You Act in the Home

Pastor Harold Clayton once said, "If you can be a Christian in the home, you can be one anywhere." I believe the statement to be true in that God desires us to be loving spouses, walking in the Spirit, 24 hours a day, 7 days a week.

The strength of our Christianity is not measured by our activity in the church, willingness to volunteer (I Corinthians 13:3), excitement during worship, or our rote knowledge of the scriptures. (I Corinthians 13:2) The quality of our walk is better determined by our ability to exhibit biblical love on a day- to-day basis in the home. (John 13:35)

Honestly, if we want to find out how filled we are with the Holy Spirit, we should not ask our pastor. We should probably start by asking our children or our spouse. They are well acquainted with a true reading of our spiritual temperature.

The Mistakes of One Generation Directly Affect the Next

Marriage is the axle to which every other spoke in our society and church are connected. When it is broken, the rest of the wheel will cease to turn.

One of the major spokes affected by a difficult marriage is that of parenting. Below, I have listed a few of the ways that children are negatively affected by either a bad marriage or divorce in general:

1. A bad marriage will negatively affect a child's level of joy and happiness.

Look at the following quote that I found a few years ago:

> "When a sample of children were asked recently in a survey what they would do if they ruled the world, they answered: 'Ban Divorce.'"[2]

Divorce is unnatural for us in that, from the beginning, we were not made to experience its effects. It was only after Adam and Eve sinned that mankind was forced to deal with the tragedy of divorce and marital disunity.

God created us to experience nothing but the perfect love of a father and mother dwelling together in unity. Thus, anything but that will produce feelings of insecurity and despair in the hearts of children.

The love and unity that husbands and wives are to have between themselves serves as an umbrella for the souls of their children. When parents fail to get along, this umbrella is removed and the hearts of their children are exposed to the elements of pain, suffering, and insecurity.

Author Michael Pearl wrote, "As the joy of the Lord is the Christian's strength, the joy of the parent is the child's strength."[3] If this is true, then it should be of no surprise that the emotional, spiritual, and mental state of our children is waning.

2. A troubled marriage will make it more difficult for children to walk in a godly manner.

In Malachi 2:15, the Lord speaks of the marriage covenant. In this passage, He tells us one of the many reasons as to why He instituted marriage:

> *"And did not he make one? . . . And wherefore one?*
> *That he might seek a godly seed."*

Malachi's message should give us some insight as to why we have such an attack on the institution of marriage in our day. It is utterly demonic in origin, in that the evil one knows that if he can destroy the institution of marriage, he will also hamper the ability of our children and our children's children to walk in a godly fashion.

Regarding divorce, Malachi 2:15 shows us that there is much more at stake than being inconvenienced by custody issues and visitation rights. According to Malachi, there is a direct correlation between a parent's ability to walk in unity with their spouse and their children's propensity to walk with the Lord.

3. When a Dad and Mom divorce, it makes it that much easier for the next generation to follow suit.

In the book of Genesis, we find that Abraham struggled with deception on two separate occasions. (Genesis 12:11-20 and Genesis 20:1-2) Isaac, just a few chapters later, followed in the footsteps of his father. (Genesis 26:6-7) Not too long after, Jacob is seen deceiving his own father, Isaac. (Genesis 27:18-19)

King David fought many a battle in his life, in which he won a valiant fight. Yet, on one occasion, he fought a battle with his flesh in which he was surprisingly not the victor. This defeat took place when he committed adultery with Bathsheba in II Samuel 11:1-5.

Interestingly enough, David had a son called Solomon, who was also a king, and his downfall was, in part, due to women. (I Kings 11:1-2)

Of a truth, more is caught than taught, and children are more likely to go in the direction that you lead rather than the direction you point. That being the case, I like to encourage couples with children to ask themselves a soul-searching question:

"Do we want our children to have the type of marriage that we currently have?"

If the answer is in the negative, then it is yet another reason to seek the Lord and His wisdom concerning your marriage.

One day, you will be sitting at a family reunion, and you will either rejoice, or have regret over the state of your children and grandchildren. In my book on anger, Angry Without a Cause, I state that "the best time to have an effect upon your grandchildren is while you are rearing your own."

Though there is no magic potion to ensure that all will be perfect in generations to come, I have found that the more work you do now as a parent usually means the less work that you and your posterity will have to do at a later time.

When divorce and dysfunction occur in one generation, it helps to desensitize the next to its ill effects. Many children are not given much of a chance to develop an emotional appetite for love, respect, and peace in the home, as they have been spoon-fed anger and hostility during their childhood. This is detrimental in that many of our children view divorce and dysfunction as a very normal part of life. In my view, once this occurs, the cycle of divorce will easily perpetuate itself for generations to come, until someone establishes a new normal in Christ.

Divorce is Costly

Why is divorce so demanding on the human body and mind? Out of all the things a person can experience, how is it that divorce nearly tops the list as being the most difficult? The answer can be found in the teachings of scripture.

Even in a troubled marriage, husbands and wives become "one flesh." We see this taught in Genesis 2:24. Howbeit, when a separation or divorce is looming, couples will start to feel a death taking place in the deepest part of their soul. This is due to the fact that as a result of becoming one, as the marriage dies, a part of them dies also.

When marriages die, both husband and wife are living witnesses to their own funeral. In fact, if there was an obituary to a divorce, both would be listed as the deceased and the survivors at the same time.

If all this were not bad enough, divorcees find themselves dealing with the stench of the corpse of their marriage for months and, sometimes, years to come. This transpires as they are often forced to deal with the other at graduations, family reunions, holiday events, and drop off locations.

I realize that this all seems rather dark, but if it feels gloomy it is only because it is gloomy. And, couples will do well to do everything within their power to fight off the death of their marriage.

Thought-Provoking Questions:

1. What is your "why behind your what?" That is, in your heart of hearts, what is your primary purpose in marriage?

2. From God's perspective, what is the purpose of marriage? (I Corinthians 10:31, Colossians 1:16, and Revelation 4:11) Can we expect His blessings in marriage if we are not living with His purpose in mind?

3. If your primary purpose in marriage is only to be happy, how can this lead to a diminished level of stamina in a troubled marriage?

4. What are some goals that you can set and meet every day, no matter what your spouse does or does not do?

5. Do you go through your day thinking that if your spouse would change, then you would be happy?

6. Do the promises of God concerning your joy and peace hinge upon your spouse's obedience to God? (Psalm 16:11, Romans 14:17, and Romans 15:13)

7. Is the source of your joy the Lord or your spouse?

8. Do you wake up happy, despite the behavior of your spouse?

9. According to I Timothy 3:15, what is one of the roles of the church? How is your lifestyle and your marriage helping that role to be fulfilled?

10. Does your immediate family see you exhibiting the fruit of the Spirit? (Galatians 5:22-23)

11. Do others outside of your home have a higher regard for your Christianity than your immediate family members?

12. How does divorce negatively affect a child's level of joy and happiness?

13. According to Malachi 2:15, what is another reason why God instituted the marriage covenant?

Closing Prayer

Lord, please forgive us for pursuing
our own happiness before Your glory.
Help us to enjoy marriages that cause
our children as well as others
to be attracted to You.

Chapter 2

WHY SO MANY TROUBLED MARRIAGES?

A Lack of God

It is impossible in a marriage for both to grow closer to Christ and not to one another. We can easily extract this principle from I John 1:7, as it states:

> *"But if we walk in the light, as he is in the light, we have fellowship one with another . . ."*

The word "we" in the above mentioned verse is a plural pronoun that can be applied to two people in a marriage. The scriptures are showing us that if two people walk close to Christ, they will have much more than a judicial relationship. They will also enjoy an intimate fellowship with one another.

A few years ago, my wife, Melody, and I came to the conclusion that the Holy Spirit will always get along with Himself. In fact, we started to see that if we were not getting along, either one of us or both of us were not walking in the Spirit.

I am not so sure that people have marriage problems as much as they have spiritual problems. Once again, the Holy Spirit will always get along with Himself, therefore, the greater need in any relationship is not so much to get along with one another as it is to get along with God.

In Ephesians 4:2, the Apostle Paul commanded the church to "keep the unity of the Spirit." I believe it is beneficial to notice that their commonality was not based upon themselves, but rather the Holy Spirit. It is also crucial to see that, in subsequent verses, Paul went on to teach the reason that the church should enjoy such unity. In Ephesians 4:4-6, Paul said:

> *"There is one body, and one Spirit, even as ye are*
> *called in one hope of your calling; One Lord, one*
> *faith, one baptism, One God and Father of all,*
> *who is above all, and through all, and in you all."*
> *(Ephesians 4:4-6)*

Paul was teaching that if God is one, then believers walking in God's Spirit should be able to move as one. This is because it is impossible for God to have disunity with Himself.

Couples that are struggling to find their way should understand that in all their attempts to solve their marriage problems, they should not leave off learning about Christ. Instead of simply trying to find commonality in mutual attraction or personal interests, they will do much better to endeavor to enjoy the unity that can only be found in the Holy Spirit.

Some may be inclined to feel this approach to be too simplistic. However, after years of helping couples in need, as a pastor and marriage speaker, I have come to the conclusion that the Holy Spirit is the missing link in most marriages today. In fact, if your home is devoid of God, then no matter how much you excel in other areas, your home will always be incomplete in some form or fashion. God created marriage so that it only functions at optimum capacity with Him at the very center.

Never did a couple enjoy a better marriage than our first parents, Adam and Eve. In the Garden of Eden, they were filled with God, therefore, they enjoyed a perfect unity. It was not until they fell out of relationship with God that fear and despair entered the scene.

Some may bristle at the very spiritual emphasis of this book. Others may be biding their time until I start to deal with more practical areas. Be that as it may, I am under an obligation to the truth to teach that if you fail in the area of walking with the Lord, you will seldom pass in others.

As you will see in chapters to come, I am more than willing to provide practical advice on overcoming marital strife. The Bible is full of such counsel. Yet, ultimately, every reader should understand that Christ said in John 15:5, ". . . without me, ye can do nothing." Therefore, the things that we are going to discuss are not necessarily hard, as much as they are impossible without the help and aid of the Holy Spirit.

Herein, by the way, lies the fundamental difference between psychology and true Christianity: psychology can sometimes tell you the right things to do, but only

Christianity can give you the power to put those things into practice.

Everything that marriage conference speakers, books on marriage, and Christian counselors say that your marriage needs can be found in the Holy Spirit. Carefully peruse the following verse from Galatians. As you read, ask yourself this question: what more does my marriage need outside of what is listed?

> *"But the fruit of the Spirit is love, joy, peace, longsuffering, gentleness, goodness, faith, meekness, temperance [self-control]. . ." (Galatians 5:22-23)*

If every person started exhibiting the fruit of the Spirit as outlined in Galatians, we would see a drastic decline in marriage issues. Books on marriage and relationships would stop selling, counselors would be looking for work, and marriage conferences would lack attendees.

If two people are lost and separated by distance, there is only one way they will ever be together again. They must focus on traversing to the same destination.

Likewise, I John 1:7 tells us that if husbands and wives will focus not so much on getting back together, but getting back to God, they will find their way back to one another.

A Lack of Light

My wife and I have six children. When they were little, we would leave for long trips in the middle of the night so as to avoid any needless stops.

Imagine during one of those midnight excursions if I decided to drive without my headlights. Would that be a wise move? Though the answer is quite obvious, what about the countless number of families that are driving without the light of God's Word in their home? (Psalm 119:13, John 8:12, and Psalm 119:105) Is there any wonder that multitudes of marriages are crashing and burning in this dark world of sin and selfishness?

A Lack of Commitment

The words commitment, duty, and obligation almost seem to carry a negative spirit with them in our day. Yet, it must be noted that they are an essential element to enjoying God's blessings, especially in marriage.

Proverbs 28:20 states that "a faithful man shall abound with blessings." Though this is applicable to many areas of our lives, it is especially pertinent when dealing with marriage.

A few years ago, a study was done among couples that stated they were unhappy in their marriages. The researchers decided to wait five years and question those that had stuck it out, in comparison to those that had thrown in the marriage towel. Out of the couples that decided to stick it out, 80 percent stated that they were happy in their marriage. Out of the people that had given up and divorced, only 19 percent said that they were happier after their divorce.[4]

As one can see from the previous statistic, commitment is not our enemy. It is a vital friend, in that the winds of convenience and emotion will often lead us away from God's best.

A Lack of Respect for the Marriage Covenant

Frankly, I am surprised to see the number of couples that call themselves Christians that view divorce as a viable option to their marriage issues. If you will receive it, I would like to make what some will deem to be a rather strong statement:

> The only differences between outright adultery and a number of our divorce and remarriage situations, are time and a piece of paper filed in divorce court.

If you carefully read the gospels, you will find that Jesus mentioned marriage on just a few occasions. But, when He did, He often related divorce and remarriage to adultery. We find these accounts in Matthew's gospel:

> *"But I say unto you, That whosoever shall put away his wife, saving for the cause of fornication, causeth her to commit adultery: and whosoever shall marry her that is divorced committeth adultery." (Matthew 5:32)*

> *"And I say unto you, Whosoever shall put away his wife, except it be for fornication, and shall marry another, committeth adultery: and whoso marrieth her which is put away doth commit adultery." (Matthew 19:9)*

We often ask, "What Jesus would do?". As a Bible teacher, I take the question a little further and wonder what His sermons would be like if He were alive today. In Matthew 5 and 19, we have an example of how Jesus would teach in relation to marriage, and it is quite the contrast to our marriage messages today. The very topic that we conveniently overlook was front and center in Christ's teachings.

When Jesus dealt with marriage, His goal was not laughter, tear-jerking stories, or countless explanations as to why couples struggle to get along. His intent was for people to view divorce and remarriage from God's perspective. Part of Christ's motive was to remind people that a light view of marriage leads to the heavy sin of adultery.

Even as I write these words, I am confident that a few will be tempted to categorize these words as archaic, old-fashioned, or legalistic. Keep in mind, I have simply quoted the God that we all claim to serve, and the same Jesus that said, "whosoever believeth in me shall not perish," also exclaimed the previous verses.

Childlike Behavior

I often tell people that as a pastoral care counselor, I am picking up where Dad and Mom left off. That is, the number one thing that I do as a pastor, life coach, and a marriage speaker is move people out of a feelings-dominated life and into a principle-driven life. In essence, I am teaching them what they failed to learn as children.

Children are motivated by feelings. That is their primary rule of law. That being said, a person has never really entered adulthood if they have not learned to follow biblical principles in spite of where their feelings are leading them.

Unfortunately, a good number of our married couples are little people in big people's bodies. Though they have secured a decent education and established a nice career, they stopped growing emotionally a long time ago. When they feel angry, they act angry. If they feel like pouting, negative behavior ensues. This is nothing less than childish behavior, and, sad to say, it is what keeps me busy as a pastor and marriage coach.

I have found that until someone learns to say yes to biblical principles and no to their childish emotions, they will never learn how to properly deal with their marital issues. They will be up one day, and down the next, and they will take their marriage on a perpetual rollercoaster ride.

Thought-Provoking Questions:

1. Can God be at disunity with Himself? (Ephesians 4:1-6) If not, then would you agree that the greatest need for couples is to walk in His Spirit?

2. In making attempts to have a great marriage, has your focus been more on getting back together with your spouse or getting back to God?

3. According to I John 1:7, it is impossible for two people to grow closer to Christ and not to one another. Do you believe this? If so, how do your actions portray your belief in this principle? That is, are you actively seeking a deeper relationship with Christ through prayer, meditation in the Word, and biblical teaching?

4. As a spouse, do you exhibit the fruit of the Spirit as listed in Galatians 5:22-23?

5. Have you been trying to fix your marriage without the Holy Spirit? Would you agree that if every marriage exhibited the fruit of the Spirit, our divorce rate would drastically decline?

6. What is the fundamental difference between psychology and Christianity?

7. Do you and your spouse endeavor to walk in the Light of God's Word? Can you think of areas where the Light of God's Word could help you to keep from stumbling in the darkness of sin and self-centeredness?

8. Do you feel that our society respects the marriage covenant? Do you view the marriage covenant as God views it?

9. Marriage has a way of making the most sophisticated of people act like little children. What type of childish behavior have you been guilty of exhibiting in your marriage? (I Corinthians 13:11)

Closing Prayer

Lord, help us to see that the
ultimate need in our marriages is to
turn toward You in repentance and faith.
Help us to realize our need to
set aside will power and utilize
the greatest power of all, the Holy Spirit.
Complete our marriages in our churches
and our land with You as every home
without Christ is incomplete.

Chapter 3

How Good Relationships Go Bad

In the early stages of a romantic relationship, couples can act according to how they feel. This is because both see the good, but not so much the bad or the ugliness of one another, as of yet. Thus, since they feel happy and hopeful that the other person is the one for them, both usually act in a kind and affectionate manner.

During the early part of a relationship, there is also a sense of newness and curiosity in the air which helps to produce a decent amount of intoxicating feelings. Though negative characteristics about the relationship and one another may be present, many are too drunk with their own emotions during this leg to notice or do anything about it.

At this juncture, when couples say, "I love you," they typically mean, "I love what you are doing for me," or, "I love the way I am feeling." They are not so much in love with meeting the needs of the other person as they are with their feelings of intoxication. Bear in mind, there is a difference.

Gradually, things change. It can be before the wedding day or after, but the atmosphere surrounding the relationship starts to feel a little different. Differences in personalities, negative behaviors and attitudes, or disagreements on how to deal with life in general start to cause the flood of emotions to subside. As these emotional waters lower, the rubble of their differences and their selfish tendencies are often in plain sight.

It is at this time that couples tend to believe that their love is waning. On the contrary, it is just now when they are going to show whether or not they have an ability to truly love each other in a biblical manner. (John 15:13 and I John 3:18) In essence, they have come to what I call the pivot point.

The Pivot Point

The pivot point is a stage that every couple comes to whether they realize it or not. It is at this phase that they either make or break their marriage or pre-marriage relationship, and they usually end up doing one of the following: quitting, fighting, settling into a chasm of mediocrity, or making the appropriate changes necessary.

The pivot point occurs when couples start to sense their initial emotions for each other waning. The feelings that once flowed so freely start to become dammed up by arguments, boredom, temper tantrums, feelings of insecurity, or the reality of what makes a relationship really work. Though this shift can come in all shapes and sizes and in different degrees, it will happen in any relationship.

Up to this time, it worked for both parties to act according to their feelings, as they previously felt happy, vulnerable, and like little kids around each other. Now, the atmosphere is different in that their emotions are minced with feelings of anger, apathy, bitterness, fear, disappointment, confusion, or possibly dejection. If they continue to act according to how they feel, they will simply make matters worse, and their relationship will fail to move to higher ground.

For couples in such a case, a change in their approach to the relationship will be necessary. In other words, when they see their initial emotions for each other changing, it is vital that they make the right pivot or change in the relationship in order to keep their feelings flowing in a positive direction. The change is as follows:

> Instead of allowing their actions to be a slave to their feelings, couples must learn to make their feelings subservient to biblical behavior.

The God of Your Marriage

When your spouse irritates you, how do you feel? Better yet, how do you respond as a result of those feelings? If you feel angry, do your words and your tone of voice follow suit? If you feel cold, indifferent, or lackluster toward your spouse, do your actions and your words portray those feelings? If the answer is yes, then I can safely say that you are in a feelings-dominated marriage and your actions are a servant to your feelings. (Romans 6:16)

If it is your habit to follow your feelings when your spouse frustrates you, then you may need to understand that your feelings are the god of your marriage. And, they are taking the place of biblical principles, as well as the leadership of the Holy Spirit. That is, if you submit to feelings of anger, malice, coldness, apathy, or bitterness, the Holy Spirit is not your master at that particular time as much as your feelings.

In Philippians 3:19, Paul addressed those that are ruled by the passions of their flesh as he wrote of those "whose God is their belly."

If you study the passage in Philippians 3, you will find that Paul was plainly speaking of people that are religious in nature, yet self-deceived. Though dreadfully religious, they follow the passions of their body instead of the God they claim to serve.

In the context of an argument or a spat with your spouse, do you adhere to biblical principles concerning love, kindness, and patience, or do you allow your feelings of negativity to dictate your behavior? If you admit to the latter, then your god during marital conflict is not Jesus and His principles. It is, as Paul taught, the passions of your flesh.

I often meet Christians that are confused because their version of Christianity has little effect upon their marriage. They are active in church and faithful to serve, yet they feel slightly bewildered because their marriage seems almost unaffected by their faith. Could it be that though these very same people know Christ, they have never learned to move contrary to their feelings of negativity? Is it possible that when dealing with their spouse, the true god of their actions is not the True God, but rather the god of self?

Wedding Vows

Imagine attending a wedding in which the groom and the bride exchanged wedding vows like this:

"I will love, honor, and cherish you when I feel like it."

I believe we would see confused looks on the faces of the attendees. They would be whispering to one another, "You had better keep your receipts as this one is never going to last!"

Though the illustration seems rather ridiculous, I believe it is an outright reality in probably 90 percent of marriages today. In my estimation, it is the primary reason as to why our divorce rate is amazingly high.

Whether we realized it or not, we signed up to have a principle-driven relationship with our spouse. When we covenanted together, we agreed to say yes to biblical principles and no to fleshly desires and feelings.

Tucked away in the traditional marriage vows is that little phrase, "for better or for worse." In essence, this means regardless of how you are feeling or what you deem to be getting out of the relationship, you agreed to love the other person in an unconditional manner.

Which marriage vows are you living out? The vows mentioned in the almost comical illustration or the traditional wedding vows? If you feel angry, apathetic, cold, rude, or even hostile and you act accordingly, then I believe the answer is obvious. It may be time to recognize that obedience to your marriage vows is obedience to God, and obedience to God is always the best and the only option worth choosing.

A Biblical Order

If you have little feelings for your spouse, it is vital to understand that feelings have no engine of their own. For the most part, feelings are pulled around by thoughts and actions. Therefore, if you are going to see a change in the way you feel about your spouse, then, first of all, you will have to change the way you are treating them. This is why I often say, "Never expect to feel any different about your marriage unless you are willing to do something different."

I have come across many a spouse that seems to be waiting for their feelings to mysteriously change before they start treating their mate in a different manner. The only problem is that they are waiting for something that does not exist.

Proverbs 16:3 gives us some insight on this subject. It tells us to:

> *"Commit thy works unto the Lord,*
> *and thy thoughts shall be established."*

If you will notice, God's Words tells us that the external can positively affect the internal. In other words, Proverbs is teaching us that in order to move the inside, sometimes the outside must be the first to change.

Imagine if I obtained a train car, painted the word "feelings" on it, and set it all by itself on the tracks. Let us also go a little further and assume that it is hundreds of miles away from where I would want it to travel.

First off, this train car may describe some of you, in that your feelings for your spouse may be far away from where they once were at another time in your marriage.

Secondly, the train car may also portray how you feel, in that you sense that you are all alone and emotionally stuck.

The question is how are we going to get that train car to move in a positive direction? We could sit back and wait for it to move on its own accord, yet I am sure that would accomplish little. We could have long conversations about possible solutions, but that would also be to no avail.

Ultimately, the only plausible way for forward progress to begin is to hook an engine to that train car and proceed down the tracks.

In like manner, husbands and wives that are seeing very little movement in their feelings toward one another must find a similar engine. I call it an engine called "action." Once positive action occurs, it is almost always just a matter of time before they start to feel differently toward one another.

As an aside, I certainly understand that there are people with chemical imbalances, hormonal problems, or physiological issues that may throw their feelings off. I am fully aware of such cases. I also understand that there are heart issues such as hurt, unforgiveness, and bitterness that take time to heal. Nevertheless, I have found that even in the most difficult of cases, there is always some way to start showing kindness so that a spouse can eventually start to feel differently about their marriage. It is not only a biblical step, but I have also found it to be extremely effective.

24 Hours a Day

It is very common to hear people say something to the effect of:

"I really don't feel like I'm in love anymore."

"I love my spouse, but I'm not ready to give my all to the marriage right now."

"I know my spouse loves me, but they are just having a hard time showing it."

I spend most of my days deprogramming people from what they have learned about love by way of the television, high school and college social scenes, music, et cetera. Let us be sure to understand that the prevailing principle of the day is that love is a feeling that gives you goose bumps or makes you tingle inside. The only problem is that this has very little to do with God's definition of love, and since God is the very essence of love, (I John 4:8) I would recommend siding with Him on the subject.

I John 3:18 and John 3:16 show us that love is about sacrifice more than mere sentiment. These verses teach us that love is portrayed by giving, not feeling. John says:

"My little children, let us not love in word, neither in tongue; but in deed and in truth." (I John 3:18)

"For God so loved the world, that he gave his only begotten Son, that whosoever believeth in him should not perish, but have everlasting life." (John 3:16)

That said, we should all understand that no matter how we feel about our spouses, we can love them 24 hours a day and 7 days a week. And, when people say, "I do not love my spouse anymore," they are really saying, "I am choosing not to love them anymore."

Thought-Provoking Questions

1. At what point did your relationship with your mate come to what I call, the pivot point?

2. When your relationship with your spouse came to the pivot point, did both of you make the correct pivot or change, or did you continue allowing your emotions to drive the relationship?

3. During the tense moments of your relationship, what has been the true God or god of your marriage? Has it been the Lord and His principles regarding emotions of anger, hostility, or apathy, or unbiblical philosophies? (Philippians 3:19 and Romans 6:16)

4. Does your marriage follow the vows in the hypothetical wedding ceremony or do both of you love in an unconditional manner?

5. Do you see how the ridiculous illustration is actually a reality in many marriages today?

6. Does the train car illustration mirror your thoughts and feelings about your marriage? That is, are your feelings for your spouse far away from where they should be? If so, what are you doing to ensure that you will feel differently about your spouse and marriage?

7. Proverbs 16:3 tells us that the external can positively affect the internal. What are some things you can do in your marriage to help you feel better about your marriage? (Proverbs 16:3)

8. If love is defined by what we do for our spouse, can you see how movies and romance novels have warped our view of what true love is? (Romans 12:2)

9. If someone is saying that they do not love their spouse anymore, then are they not simply stating that they are choosing not to love them anymore? (John 3:16 and I John 3:18)

10. If we can love our spouse 24 hours a day regardless of our feelings, then what are some things that you can do to show forth love in your relationship?

Closing Prayer:

Lord, help us to better perform our marriage vows.
Give us the power to love the other in the marriage
in a way that only You can supply.

Chapter 4

THE TOP MISTAKE
MEN MAKE IN A FIGHT

When husbands and wives feel a fight coming on, both have a unique way of making battle preparations. While the man loads his cannon of logic, the woman looks to her emotions as a means of defense. It is not too long before both are involved in a battle that has raged throughout the ages between many a husband and wife. It is a battle that has produced few, if any, victors, yet many casualties.

As the man fires what he deems to be reasonable statements, the woman builds a castle of emotions around herself to thwart off the attack. What happens from here is classic, yet tragic.

The man muses within himself, "To successfully storm the castle, I must shoot more cannon balls of facts and logical surmisings over this wall." Forgetting that logic based upon false premises is foolishness, he fires away only to have missed one of the most crucial facts of all. No man in the history of marriage has ever been able to scale the heights of that wall. For the more cannon balls of logic and reason that he tries to fire over her wall, it only grows in height and in thickness.

It is at this juncture that many men falter. They do not fail in what they are saying, for their logic is fairly factual. Their failure lies more in when and how they are trying to convey their thoughts.

The wise man realizes that the said wall of emotion is a temporary wall. He understands that time will erode it away, if he chooses to serve in the moment and convince at a later time. Unfortunately, many men do the exact opposite. Instead of serving now and convincing later, many make the mistake of thinking they will serve their wife once they get everything worked out on an intellectual basis. The problem is that after 6,000 years of world history, this method has proved to be ineffectual.

Proverbs 18:19 also gives us further insight on this matter as it states that "a brother offended is harder to be won than a strong city." It goes on to say that "their contentions are like the bars of a castle." To put it simply, the verse it teaching us that when a person's spirit is wounded or closed, it is near impossible to gain entrance to the rest of their being.

This is key in that when a person's spirit is closed to us, we feel that the best way to reach them is to enter through the back door of their intellect. The problem with this thought process is that Proverbs tells us otherwise. In essence, Proverbs 18:19 is telling us that a person's spirit acts almost as a gate to their respective city. If it is closed, it is improbable that you will gain access any other way. Therefore, in order to access someone's mind, you must first open their spirit, and this is best accomplished through sacrificial service rather than carefully constructed arguments.

This teaching will not come easy for the man or the woman that likes to deal with things in the here and now. If you are like me, when there is a problem in a relationship, you want it fixed yesterday. The only issue is that you are not married to yourself. More than likely, you are married to someone that has an entirely different way of processing their emotions and their thoughts.

Many a couple will avoid a multitude of late night arguments and free-for-alls by taking heed to this advice. Instead of stomping off and declaring the other person to be absolutely unreasonable, they will find it more effective to serve now and convince at a later time. This usually allows time for that wall of emotion to crumble and the spirit of the other to open. Once this occurs, a spouse will usually have access to the other's intellect, and they will be able to discuss a matter on a more rational basis.

Mud Pit

Women sometimes find themselves in what I call an emotional mud pit. There are times when their men have pushed them in, and there are times when few know how they landed in such a place. Regardless, a man's response in such a case will prove to be vital to his success or failure as a husband.

Many men are bad about using the come along or winch of reason and logic to pull their wives out of such a pit. I have found that this only exacerbates an already difficult situation as women usually end up becoming even more stuck when men attempt to use such methods.

Proverbs 15:2 is an extremely applicable verse to quote regarding this issue. It says:

"The tongue of the wise useth knowledge aright: but the mouth of fools poureth out foolishness."

I have always felt this to be an extraordinary verse because it differentiates between being right and acting in a wise manner. It shows us that though we are sometimes factual, we may not be wise in how we handle what we know to be true.

Many couples die on a battlefield of rightness. Holding to their hard facts and high ideals, they will often march right over a cliff of rightness to the ruin of their relationship. This is why some have said that couples should decide whether they want to be right or have a great marriage.

Men are often factual in what they are saying to their wives, but not necessarily wise in how and when they say it. When their wives are in a difficult emotional state, the better approach is to use the come along of unconditional love and kindness rather than that of logic and reason. This usually allows time to dry that emotional mud pit, and, at a later time, they can choose to relate their talking points if they still feel the need. However, in the moment, it is usually better to keep quiet and sacrificially serve.

This all brings me to a very good point. Most couples argue about things that will matter very little to them in five minutes. This is one of the major reasons as to why couples should learn to table a conversation until a later time. It is because much of what couples argue about will be of little concern when they are outside of the emotions of a situation.

Once couples are emotionally involved in a discussion, there is little good to follow. This is because once offended, they tend to put on what I call the sunshades of negativity. The problem hereafter is that no matter how bright their statements are with logic and good intentions, the other person views them through the lenses of anger and frustration. After this occurs, little good will follow.

Role Reversal

Verbalizing heart issues is often a difficult task. In trying to help the masses, there are some couples whose paradigm is slightly different from most. For this reason, I would like to address an exception to the previous two sections.

Much of our counseling on marriage seems to deal with the aggressive male that is so into himself that he fails to stay in touch with the emotional needs of his delicate wife. Though this is certainly worth addressing, some couples have what I would call a role reversal, in that it is the wife that is more aggressive in nature in comparison to her more passive husband.

For marriages in such a state, it should be noted that the woman can often be just as guilty as the man when it comes to using logic and reason to penetrate walls of emotion. As the wife verbalizes what she deems to be very logical statements about the past, the husband will often run for cover in what I call an emotional or physical cave. Couples that find themselves in this scenario will do well to apply many of the same rules as previously mentioned, yet with a few considerations:

1. Though I usually stress that is it vital for men to learn to serve now and convince later, the more passive male may need to serve his wife by showing up for conversation. In these situations, ninety percent of success for the male is usually showing up for the talks that the wife desires to have. Bear in mind, these talks should never take place with a wall of emotion between the two.

2. Usually the more passive male is married to a woman that is far superior at articulating her thoughts. Men married to women as such often feel verbally backed into a corner during fights and arguments. The wise woman in this type of a marriage should be careful to talk to her husband in a way that does not make him feel demeaned or less like a man.

Thought-Provoking Questions:

1. Does the castle illustration at the beginning of this chapter describe your arguments or discussions with your spouse?

2. Who in your relationship is prone to fire the cannon balls of logic and reason?

3. Have you or your spouse been guilty of trying to open the other person's intellect before their spirit?

4. What are some ways that you can serve your spouse so as to open their spirit?

5. Do you or your spouse struggle to table a matter until a later time?

6. Proverbs 15:2 tells us that we can be factual yet still unwise in how we deal with our spouses. Have you or your spouse been right yet wrong in how and when you discuss a matter?

7. Have you and your spouse been guilty of arguing about matters that will mean very little to you five minutes or hours later?

8. When your spouse is in an emotional mud pit, what are some things that you do or say that cause them to be even more emotionally stuck?

9. Is there a role reversal in your marriage as described in the previous chapter?

10. If you are a more passive male, are there times when you would rather hide in an emotional or a physical cave than deal with an issue?

11. Are you a wife married to a more passive male? Do you have times when your words cause him to feel backed into a corner or inferior?

Closing Prayer:

Lord, give us wisdom to open the spirit of our spouse before attempting to reach their intellect. Help us to be wise as well as right in our discussions.

Chapter 5

THE BRIDGE

For a woman, marriage is a bridge upon which she desires to safely walk. If that bridge has ever fallen through, she thinks twice before bearing all her weight on it again.

Most women want to know that their relationship with their husband is stable in the areas of unconditional love, commitment, emotional intimacy, and finances. Deep down, they desire to know that this bridge called marriage will hold up their sense of self worth as well as their expectations. When it shows signs of weakness, they tend to test its strength by doing what I call jumping up and down. This is usually done in one or more of the following ways:

1. A wife may withhold her love for her husband until she sees that he truly cares about her and not merely himself.

2. She may show hesitancy to act like everything is fine in the marriage.

3. Some act cold or indifferent about the marriage until they see viable change.

4. A wife might question her husband's motives for making changes for the better.

5. A woman could display a lack of willingness to participate in physical intimacy.

6. She could be curt, and, at times, rude toward her husband.

These are all natural tendencies for a wife that feels insecure about her relationship with her husband. This, of course, does not condone this type of behavior, but it certainly explains why some wives are tempted to act in such a way.

Many a man has found himself standing on a broken down, dilapidated bridge called marriage, trying to encourage his wife to follow. While he stands wooing, begging, and, sometimes, pleading with his wife to trust him once more, she often reacts with reluctance. It's not so much her reluctance or lack thereof that will determine their success, as much as his reaction to her reluctance that will be key.

Some men, while standing on that bridge, feel either afraid or overwhelmed by the task. Others feel incapable. Either way, they will do well not to run and hide from their God-given responsibility to promote an atmosphere of safety in their marriage through sacrificial service and safe conversation.

Other men err in that they focus on their wife's reluctance rather than their responsibility to strengthen the bridge with the planks of unconditional love and biblical character. This is a crucial mistake that many, if not most, men make.

Early in our marriage, I was guilty of such behavior. Rather than rebuilding the bridge of trust through unconditional love and kindness, I was more focused on the thought of my wife jumping up and down. This only served to delay any type of substantial success.

As a young married man, I would try to use my carefully constructed arguments and long lectures to reassure my wife, Melody, that the bridge would never fall through again. Looking back, I could have avoided countless one-sided discussions by doing more to repair the bridge than trying to sell her on the state of it.

When women show hesitancy to trust their husbands, men often become defensive. Although this is a natural reaction for most men, it will do little to boost a woman's level of confidence. Men that are prone to this behavior will be wise to understand that there is a formula for rebuilding trust. I call it, change over time.

Men usually do not mind the numerator of my formula. Change is sometimes easy. It is the denominator of the equation that causes most to struggle.

When men repent or change their minds, they often change on the spot by making an about-face turn. Women, on the other hand, are vastly different in that they reverse directions by making a very slow 180 degree turn. This is often a tremendous source of frustration to men trying to woo their wives.

As we saw in the last chapter, when a woman is hurt, she will often build a castle around her heart and shut the door tight. As she hides out for safety, it is vital that the man patiently serve as he waits for her to open that door. Any signs of impatience will send out a resounding message that he is serving his fears rather than her needs. She will also be prone to perceive that he is simply using the date nights, flowers, and charitable acts of kindness as a form of control to get her to conform to his wishes.

Meekness

Up to this point, some men may feel that I am encouraging them to be what some would deem henpecked in order to fix their marriage. Nothing could be further from the truth. I am not purporting that men be push-overs, as much as I am encouraging them to exercise what the Bible terms to be meekness.

Many have attempted to define meekness. I define it as such:

Meekness is appearing to lose the battle, knowing that eventually you will win the war.

Is this not why Christ was silent before Pilate in Matthew 27:11-14? As He stood before His accusers, there was no need to defend Himself. The power of God and His resurrection from the dead would come to His defense in just a few short days.

Many spouses would do well to take on the attitude of Christ and realize that meekness is not giving up the fight. It is learning to fight in a more effective way. It is appearing to take an immediate loss while laying hold of long term gains through faith and biblical conduct.

Husbands and wives should understand that love, kindness, and especially patience pave the way for effective communication at a later time. They have a way of building up what I call a bank account of credibility and trust that will allow them to make the appropriate withdrawals at a later time.

Some men may feel that unconditional love makes them to appear weak, but that is a type of mirage, for they are actually using the strongest weapon known to man.

Solomon said, "Many waters cannot quench love, neither can the floods drown it: if a man would give all the substance of his house for love, it would utterly be contemned." (Song of Solomon 8:7) In the verse before this, he also said that "love is strong as death." (Song of Solomon 8:6)

From Solomon's song, we can gather that unconditional love is the strongest weapon that a man can use when fighting for his marriage. He may appear weak in that he may have to lose a few arguments and appear to be in the wrong, but his willingness to love will only help to right a relationship previously wronged by selfish behavior.

Thought-Provoking Questions:

1. Has the bridge of your marriage every cracked or fallen through?

2. Did the bridge illustration accurately describe how both were tempted to respond?

3. How is a wife tempted to react when the bridge of her marriage has fallen through?

4. Is she willing to get right back on that bridge?

5. What are some of the planks that cause a woman to feel safe enough to walk on that bridge?

6. As a husband, have you ever found yourself focusing on your wife's reluctance rather than your responsibility to strengthen the bridge of your marriage?

7. How did this chapter define meekness? (Matthew 5:5, Matthew 27:11-14, Matthew 11:29, and Titus 3:2)

8. As a spouse, do you have a difficult time appearing to lose an argument?

9. Do you believe that unconditional love is the strongest weapon known to man? Do your actions portray that belief? (Song of Solomon 8:6-7)

Closing Prayer:

*Lord, help us to understand that the
strongest weapon known to man
is that of unconditional love.
Help us to forsake worldly philosophies
about marriage and relationships
and learn from You,
the Author of love.*

Chapter 6

KEEPING MORALE
AT A HIGH LEVEL

Right-Driven Versus
Results-Driven

Husbands and wives trying to resolve their marriage issues have a way of setting themselves up for feelings of discouragement. They do this by being what I call results-driven instead of right-driven.

Our primary objective in life should never be to get results as much as it should be to walk in obedience to God. Whenever this is turned around in our minds, we are inviting disappointment into our lives, as God seldom works on our timetable.

Solomon addressed this area in Proverbs. Proverbs 3:6 wisely counsels:

> *"In all thy ways acknowledge Him,*
> *and He shall direct thy paths."*

Notice the order in Proverb 3. Solomon tells us that our responsibility is to acknowledge God through faith and obedience to His Word. As we submit to His will,

Solomon teaches us that God will guide us into a pathway of blessing.

Unfortunately, we typically do the exact opposite of what Solomon is teaching. Our sights are usually set on what we want in life rather than Whom we should be serving. This is actually a form of disobedience, no matter how good our intentions appear to be. As Matthew Henry said, "Duty is ours, events [results] are God's."[5]

Imagine with me for a few moments that you are at the bottom of a milk jug and it is your desire to find your way to the top. Let us also assume that you only have two choices: swim to the surface or become cream which finds a way to rise to the top.

Obedience to God and spiritual character development cause us to be that cream that finds a way to rise to the top. In essence, this is what the scriptures are teaching us through Proverbs 3. As we work at being obedient to the scriptures, God promises to cause us to rise to a state of blessedness.

When endeavoring to solve marriage problems, it is best to set your sights on obedience to your marriage vows rather than how much progress you are making. At the end of the day, your goal should be to ask yourself this question:

"Did I walk in obedience to God by obeying my marriage vows?"

If the answer to that question is a resounding yes, then you will be able to find comfort in the following ways:

1. God rewards obedience regardless of what others do.

Ephesians 6:8 tells us that "whatsoever good thing any man doeth, the same shall he receive of the Lord." This is a very applicable verse to marriage in that whosoever does right, the Bible tells us that their reward does not lie in the hands of their spouse. It is in the faithful and loving hands of the Lord.

Husbands and wives that feel their happiness is controlled by their spouse are giving far too much power to their mate. Only God should hold that much power over our inward state.

Keep in mind, if your spouse has had that power over you, it is not because they have taken it. It is because you have given it away through a lack of faith or a misunderstanding of the scriptures. As stated earlier, God's promises concerning your own happiness and joy never hinge upon your spouse's obedience or disobedience to God. They only rest upon the faithfulness of the Almighty God.

2. Your future is bright no matter how your spouse acts.

Whether in this life or the life to come, God promises a blessed state to those that walk in accordance to His Word. Here are a few scriptures that validate this point:

> "... blessed are they that hear the word of God,
> and keep it." (Luke 11:28)

"Blessed is the man that walketh not in the counsel of the ungodly, nor standeth in the way of sinners, nor sitteth in the seat of the scornful. But his delight is in the law of the Lord; and in his law doth he meditate day and night. And he shall be like a tree planted by the rivers of water, that bringeth forth his fruit in his season; his leaf also shall not wither; and whatsoever he doeth shall prosper." (Psalm 1:1-3)

When it comes to your future, I do not know how or when God will fulfill the promises in Luke 11 and Psalm 1. I also cannot guarantee what type of reaction your spouse will have to the changes that you have been making in your marriage. What I do know is that God and all the blessings that come with Him are in the future of those that walk with Him, and He has promised that He "will never leave thee, nor forsake thee." (Hebrews 13:5)

Bury the Seed of Expectation

Expectations can be a manifestation of true faith in the Lord (Hebrews 11:1) or they can grow out of a selfish desire to see problems eradicated as quickly as possible. More times than naught, they are weeds that grow out of the roots of fear, greed, and impatience.

There will be some reading this book that are desperately trying to win back their spouses. These individuals usually do not err in what they are doing as much as how and when they expect their spouses to come around. Behind their random acts of kindness and words of encouragement is a heat that is burning with expectation. This is always a grave error for a number of reasons. I have listed a few of them below:

1. Higher expectations lead to greater resistance.

If you are in a troubled marriage, you are potentially in what I call hyper-fix-it mode. Fearing divorce or separation, you may be saying and doing all the right things with a great amount of intensity, but to no avail. It may seem that the harder you chase, the faster the other person runs away from you. If it appears that way, it is probably because it is so. You are the hound that is chasing the fox, in that as you up the chase, the other person runs away with even more vigor than before.

At this point, your perception is probably that the other person is unthankful, hurt beyond repair, or hard-hearted because of their unwillingness to reciprocate your love to them. It is entirely possible that you have come to the wrong conclusion. The problem may not be with their unwillingness as much as with your lack of understanding and patience.

It seems that few people see that their expectations have a way of pressurizing their marriage. They cause an air of tension in a home that is so thick that, at times, one could almost cut it with a knife. As long as this tension exists, even the most dramatic changes will be met with resistance, as no one likes to feel pressured into changing, nor do they want to be sold on the marriage.

You may be going through the day hoping that this is the day your spouse comes around and owns the marriage. Behind every kind word and loving deed is a spirit of anxiousness that is awaiting that moment when the other person falls into your arms and verbalizes their lifelong commitment to the marriage. The only problem is that this typically only exists in the movies, as people normally change here a little and there a little.

If you feel that I am hitting home, a tweak in your spirit may be in order. You will be wise to do what I call burying the seed of expectation.

I can purchase the best gardening seeds that money can buy, but if I never bury them in the ground, they are worth but little. Jesus even spoke to this end. In John 12:24, He said:

> *"Verily, verily, I say unto you, Except a corn of*
> *wheat fall into the ground and die, it abideth alone:*
> *but if it die, it bringeth forth much fruit."*

There is a sense where your expectations are like a packet of seeds. Until you bury them, you will probably fail to see much fruit.

If your spouse feels that there is an ulterior motive behind everything you do and say, you will almost always be met with some form of resistance. If they perceive that your primary objective is to remedy yourself of a problem rather than to love them unconditionally, they will resent even the most sacrificial forms of love.

2. You are presenting an unattractive view of yourself to your spouse.

When spouses have a spirit of desperation or a strong spirit of expectancy, they present an unappealing side of themselves. Their demeanor is, at best, weak and that of a freshman begging a senior for a chance to dance.

Your spouse does not need a charity case as much as a husband or wife that is gentle in spirit and strong in conviction. He or she will be more attracted to someone that is calmly and confidently serving out of a sense of obedience to God rather than a fear of losing their mate.

3. Your spouse will feel controlled.

In days gone by, some spouses served themselves through selfish behavior. Realizing the error of their ways, they repented and are now doing everything possible to repair the bridge of trust between their spouse's heart and their own. The only problem is that even though some have amended their external actions, they may be still serving themselves by catering to their fears instead of the needs of the other person.

In an odd sort of way, desperate spouses will use even biblical behavior to control the fate of their marriage. Though they are usually doing and saying all the right things, it is often with an unhealthy spirit of expectancy based in fear rather than faith. Instead of loving their spouse unconditionally, they are actually serving their fear of either losing their mate or feeling abandoned.

Usually, a man or woman in such a predicament is slightly perplexed. The confusion is brought on by the unresponsiveness of their spouse. In their mind, the other half is hard-hearted or hurt beyond repair. Many times, it is neither, as the other person feels that their spouse's motivation is skewed. Deep down, they feel that if they waiver from their defensive posture, they will be pulled around by a leash made up of good words, fair speeches, and romantic acts. In short, they are not resisting being loved as much as they are feeling controlled.

4. Your spouse will know that something is up.

I like to say that every person is a psychologist in that you may be able to lie to someone's face or manipulate their mind, but it is much harder to deceive someone's spirit. Of course, it is possible, but most of us know when something is just not quite right.

If your motivation is not that of unconditional love, your spouse will know that something is up. They may not be able to verbalize their thoughts and feelings, but they will have reason to be hesitant and, at times, extremely cautious.

Unconditional love is a great weapon. In fact, it is the strongest weapon known to man according to the Song of Solomon. But, it is possible to have a smooth stone of good behavior in a sling of self-centered expectations. If the case be so with you, then your spouse will always be hesitant to act like all is wonderful.

What to do with a Desperate Spouse

Are you living with a spouse that is working overtime to win you over? Finding it difficult to process all the changes and accept this new normal around the home? If so, you probably feel slightly overwhelmed in that as you hide in an emotional break room, requesting space, he or she craves closeness. While you look at time as a trustworthy friend, the other half views it to be their worst enemy.

How do you handle the desperate spouse that has turned over a new leaf, realized the error of their ways, and is doing everything imaginable to save the marriage? Here are a few things to consider:

1. If you wait until you feel like loving your spouse before returning their love, you may be waiting a long time.

As I previously mentioned, never expect to feel differently about your spouse, if you are not willing to do something different. (Proverbs 16:3)

2. Forgiveness always requires risk.

Some are afraid to forgive their spouse because they are waiting for that 100 percent risk-free option that they will not be hurt again. The only problem is that, as my dad says, "There is no such animal."

I do not remember the Lord ever sending an angel down with a pen and paper in hand to have me sign a written guarantee that I will never sin again before granting me forgiveness. Of course, a genuine attitude of repentance will be accompanied by a willingness to turn away from sin (Proverbs 28:13 and Isaiah 55:7), but there is not necessarily a 100 percent guarantee against it ever happening again.

If you are going to walk over the bridge of forgiveness with your spouse, you may have to accept that the bridge may collapse at some point. However, even if your husband or your wife falters and fails, it is important to comprehend that what does not make you, can never break you. Therefore, the successes nor the failures of your spouse should be the foundation of your joy and peace. If they are, then in some form or fashion, they have taken the place of God in your life.

Only God should have supreme rule over your emotions. (Psalm 18:2 and 28:7) All others, including your mate, should never enjoy that much power over you. In fact, an understanding of this principle can help to minimize the emotional risk involved with giving your spouse a second, if not a third and fourth chance. This is because another person's propensity to devastate you emotionally will only be proportionate to how much you depend upon them for emotional sustenance.

3. People tend to learn backwards.

If your spouse is pushing hard to win you back, you probably feel that their motives are off. You may be sensing that their motivation is that of fear and not so much of unconditional love. That being the case, you may feel tempted to stiff arm them until they change their motives first. I believe that this would be a mistake as, unfortunately, people tend to learn backwards. In other words, that which we should learn first, we usually learn last.

There are some things in life that start out in fear that end in love. One of which is our relationship with the Lord. Proverbs 1:7 shows us that "the fear of the Lord is the beginning of knowledge." Yet, according to Christ's teachings in Matthew 22:37-40, God's ultimate goal for His children is to have a love relationship with Him.

Some spouses may change their behavior out of a fear of losing their marriage, yet grow in the area of unconditional love at a later time. Therefore, though you may perceive that your spouse's motives are distorted, it does not mean that all is lost. It simply means that you are married to a human being that has a propensity to learn in reverse.

On a further note, it may help you to consider that if God only helped those that changed in the proper order, very few of us would ever be in a place of blessing with the Lord.

Thought-Provoking Questions:

1. Have you been working to obtain results in your marriage before focusing on obedience to God?

2. According to Proverbs 3:5-6, should our focus be on securing results, or our relationship with God?

3. Do you make it one of your main goals to eradicate your marriage problems or to obey your marriage vows?

4. Do you love your spouse without any strings attached?

5. If a spouse is serving the other, but with a high level of expectation that they will turn around, how will that hurt their cause in the end?

6. Is it possible to use even good behavior as a form of control over your spouse?

7. Have you buried the seeds of your expectations? (John 12:24)

8. Forgiveness always requires some type of risk. Are you willing to take the same risk that God takes when He grants us forgiveness?

9. As mentioned, fear is sometimes apparent before unconditional love. Are you willing to allow your spouse to learn backwards as we do with the Lord? (Proverbs 1:7 and Matthew 22:37-40)

Closing Prayer:

Lord, encourage those today
that feel like giving up.
Help them to make it their goal
to walk in obedience to You and leave
the results of their obedience in Your hands.

Chapter 7

HOW TO FIGHT FOR YOUR MARRIAGE WITHOUT FIGHTING WITH ONE ANOTHER

Great Motives, Lousy Methods

Most couples fight for their marriage in a way that hurts their relationship instead of helping it. I admit, their motives are usually honorable, but it is their methods that are less than effective.

Moses had a great motive when he came to the aid of the Hebrew slave in Exodus 2:11-12. Very few fault him for that. Howbeit, it was his use of brute force that seemed to thrust him into trouble.

Likewise, most couples have great intentions when they fight for their marriage, but they often fight in a way that wrongs the relationship and one another.

Imagine that you and your spouse are in a fort and have been given a charge to defend it. Also, bear with me a while and conjure up pictures of an enemy firing upon that fort with rifles and cannons. Would it not be rather ludicrous for the both of you to scurry to your feet, pick up your rifles, and start shooting at one another?

Unfortunately, this crude illustration is what happens in many households today. As many couples come under fire, they end up attacking one another rather than the real issues that they are facing.

When counseling, I let couples know that I have the same motives they have had all along. I just have a better and more biblical way of solving their marital issues. Instead of wielding swords that do more harm than good, I encourage them to pick up weapons that are not only condoned by the scriptures, but beneficial in solving their marital issues.

A 2-Step Process

There are a thousand ways that couples find to head toward what I call the south pole. The south pole is where anger, bitterness, resentment, a lack of communication, little or no intimacy, apathy, and emotional lethargy reside.

As a pastor, when I first started to deal with couples in need, I would spend large amounts of time trying to keep couples from taking the thousands of different paths that there are, down to the south pole. If a couple had a problem with anger, I would relate as many scriptures as possible that warn people against the use of anger. If their struggle was in the area of communication, I would attempt to give them verses detailing the woes of using ill-advised forms of communication. The only problem was that I found my counseling was only so effective. I not only found that the tone of the sessions was fairly dark, but many couples were leaving more frustrated than when they entered my office. Finally, a better, faster, and more biblical approach was discovered.

Through the course of time, I started to see that the best way to keep couples from taking the hundreds, if not thousands, of roads to the south pole was to encourage them to start heading toward the north pole. In other words, I found that if couples would focus on doing a few positive things right, by virtue of doing those few positive things, they would often stop doing the hundreds of negative things they found to do to irritate one another. This was all discovered as I considered the teachings of Christ in the gospel of Matthew.

In Matthew 22:37-40, the scriptures tell us the following:

> *"Jesus said unto him, Thou shalt love the Lord
> thy God with all thy heart, and with all thy soul,
> and with all thy mind. This is the first and great
> commandment. And the second is like unto it, Thou
> shalt love thy neighbour as thyself. On these two
> commandments hang all the law and the prophets."*

This teaching was probably mesmerizing to the average Jew in that Jesus took all of the Old Testament commands and summed them up into two positive commands. He essentially taught that by virtue of loving God and loving others, His followers would not be doing all the negative things that God said not to do in the Old Testament.

While musing on this subject, I took the time to apply this same principle in part to marriage, and I discovered something. I found that though there are definitely times when we need to hear the thou-shalt-nots of marriage, there was a more refreshing and biblical approach to helping couples. I found that if couples would concentrate on taking two positive steps, by virtue of taking those two positive steps, they would often stop doing the hundreds of negative things that they would often do to hurt the relationship. Thus, I started to teach a 2-step process to fighting for your marriage, without fighting one another.

Branches

You have probably noticed that I love to use word pictures. Jesus, the Master Teacher, set this example. That being said, I would like to relate one more illustration to you before diving into our two step process.

I liken marriage issues to a Christmas tree that is leaning in the wrong direction. If it is my job to straighten the tree, I have two ways that I can go about accomplishing that task.

The first way would be tedious and, at best, frustrating. This way would involve handling the individual branches of the tree and trying to bend them in a new direction. The other way would be the preferred option in that I could take the time to straighten the trunk or the base of the tree. The idea is that if I would straighten the base of the tree, the branches would also start pointing in the right direction.

Unfortunately, I believe that some of our modern day counseling advice falls underneath the first method, and I have found that it is an ineffective way of dealing with marital issues. The better option is usually to focus on encouraging couples to fix a few foundational issues that are causing the rest of the issues in their marriage. Our 2-step process is designed with that purpose in mind.

Not a Magic Bullet

Man has a propensity to want a magic bullet to solve life's problems. He wants something that he can quickly do or apply that will eradicate his issues apart from total obedience to God. Let me say that I do not believe that any such thing exists. In fact, the next few chapters are really not steps as much as they are an encouragement for an entire paradigm shift in your life. It is not a formula, as much as it is a set of exhortations to wholly submit your actions and your thoughts to the Lordship of Christ, by way of His Word.

Our 2-step process is not a formula as much as it is a repackaging of biblical principles. It is simply a different angle on the same Word, or we could call it the same meal served on a different platter.

Thought-Provoking Questions:

1. Like Moses, can you see ways that you and your spouse have had good motives but lousy methodology? (Exodus 2:11-12)

2. What are some methods that you and your spouse have used to solve your marriage problems that have proved to be ineffectual?

3. What are some of the paths that have led you and your spouse down to the south pole?

4. According to this chapter, what is the best way to ensure that your marriage is not heading toward the south pole?

5. Jesus summed up all of the "thou shalt nots" in the Old Testament with two positive commands. What were those commands? (Matthew 22:37-40)

6. Our 2-step process teaches couples to do a few fundamental things right. Consequently, by virtue of doing those few correct things, couples often stop doing the hundreds of negative things they find to do that irritate one another. Are you ready to learn these 2 biblical steps?

Closing Prayer:

Lord, help all that read the next few chapters to
submit their will, and, subsequently, their actions
to You for your glory and their own good.
Help them to realize that You are not a "quick fix",
but a life altering God that gives life
where there has previously been death.

Chapter 8

THE FIRST STEP
FOR THE MEN

World Class Business Client

The first step for men is to start treating their wives as they would a world class business client, regardless of how they feel or what they perceive they are getting out of the relationship.

Most readily admit that if the average man treated his business clients or associates like he has his wife in the last six months, he would either be broke or out of a job a long time ago.

If a customer, business client, or higher-up misunderstands a matter, what do most men in the business world do? Do they get critical, sarcastic, or demeaning? It is almost a rhetorical question in that those worth their salt listen with genuine concern and attentiveness. If a potential client is about to sign on the dotted line yet he starts to show apprehension, how do most men in the sales force react? They show concern and empathy, and they strive to answer their every question. Unfortunately, with many men, this willingness to please and serve, often ends with a hard day's work at the office or the job site.

For some reason, many men tend to believe it is acceptable to treat those closest to them the worst. If anything, the opposite should be the norm.

Have you ever heard someone say something cutting or rude, and then follow with something to the effect of:

"It's okay because he's like family."

Have you ever thought about what is being said when this occurs? He or she is trying to convince others that it is okay to treat someone in a less than appropriate manner as long as they are on the same level as a family member.

More than we realize, many of us have adopted the philosophy that it is perfectly normal and acceptable to treat those with whom we live with less respect than those outside of the home. It must be noted that though this is normal in our society today, it is unacceptable according to the scriptures.

Whether you are a businessman, mechanic, pastor, blue or white collar worker, when you get home, your work is just beginning. When you walk through the door of your house, it is not time to relax, as much as it is to work just as hard at pleasing your wife as most men do their cliental or business associates.

The Fundamental Problem

The fundamental problem between husbands and wives is namely this: Husbands serve themselves or their interests more than their wives, and women try to change that behavior by using means that are less than effective. Are there exceptions to this rule? Of course, but, keep in mind that the exception usually proves the rule, and, generally speaking, this is the foundational issue in most troubled marriages.

In relation to other subjects, the scriptures do not mention marriage all that much. But, when the Lord does, He certainly nails it. This is the case in Ephesians 5:28-29. This passage admonishes:

> *"So ought men to love their wives as their own bodies. He that loveth his wife loveth himself. For no man ever yet hated his own flesh; but nourisheth and cherisheth it, even as the Lord the church:"*

In Ephesians 5, we see God going after what I call the jugular of marriage problems. He is saying in a few short verses what authors and speakers take hundreds of pages to say. He is showing us that men have a tendency to be selfish and especially lazy when it comes to serving their wives. His solution is quite simple: men are to serve their wives with the same intensity level and rigor that they naturally want to serve themselves.

Regardless of How You Feel

As I stated in previous chapters, many couples have issues because their feelings of hopelessness, apathy, hurt, and anger have been their marriage counselor, guide, and even the god of their marriage. (Philippians 3:19 and Romans 6:16) Because they feel negative, they feel they have a right to act negatively. This is why I say that part of the first step for the men is to treat their wives like a world class client, regardless of how they feel.

Ephesians 5:25 sets the standard for a husband's love toward his wife. This verse says:

"Husbands, love your wives, even as Christ also loved the church, and gave himself for it;"

When we see this verse in the book of Ephesians, it is important to ask the question, "How did Christ love the church?" Granted, there are a myriad of ways to answer this question, but one of those ways can be seen in Matthew 26:36-39. This portion of scripture states:

"Then cometh Jesus with them unto a place called Gethsemane, and saith unto the disciples, Sit ye here, while I go and pray yonder. And he took with him Peter and the two sons of Zebedee, and began to be sorrowful and very heavy. Then saith he unto them, My soul is exceeding sorrowful, even unto death: tarry ye here, and watch with me. And he went a little farther, and fell on his face, and prayed, saying, O my Father, if it be possible, let this cup pass from me: nevertheless not as I will, but as thou wilt."

Matthew's gospel gives us an account of Jesus the night before the crucifixion. It provides for us a glimpse of the struggle that took place in the heart and soul of Christ.

Matthew tells us that the struggle was such that Christ did something that you only see once in His earthly walk. He prayed three times for the same answer.

In verse 39 of Matthew 26, He prayed:

> *"O my Father, if it be possible, let this cup pass from me: nevertheless not as I will, but as thou wilt."*

In the 42nd verse of the same chapter, the scriptures tell us that he prayed for a second time. This verse says:

> *"He went away again the second time, and prayed, saying, O my Father, if this cup may not pass away from me, except I drink it, thy will be done."*

Just a few verses later, the Bible tells us that he prayed for even a third time. Here is Matthew's narrative in verse 44:

> *"And he left them, and went away again, and prayed the third time, saying the same words."*

The next day, Christ was going to drink the cup of God's wrath for not only the sins of the world, but also His bride, the church. Yet, on the night before He was crucified, we see that His feelings were heavy with sorrow as He anticipated bearing the punishment for our sins. (II Corinthians 5:21, Isaiah 53:6 and 10)

At this point, I would like men to see that though Christ was experiencing negative emotions, He still submitted to doing the will of the Father concerning His bride, the church. Similarly, husbands should take on the same approach in that though their emotions may be laden with sorrow, sadness, or feelings of hopelessness, they should still choose to sacrificially serve their wives.

Also, I have often felt it hypocritical for men to receive Christ's sacrificial love yet display an unwillingness to love their wives in the same way that Christ has loved them. Once again, He loved us in spite of the pain, suffering, and even the emotional agony that was associated with the cross. Now, He asks us to love others, as well as our wives, in the same way that He has shown His love toward us.

The scriptures tell us to love others in the way that Jesus has loved us. Certainly, we could apply the scriptures mentioned below to our wives also:

"A new commandment I give unto you,
That ye love one another; as I have loved you,
that ye also love one another." (John 13:34)

"And be ye kind one to another, tenderhearted,
forgiving one another, even as God for Christ's sake
hath forgiven you." (Ephesians 4:32)

". . . walk in love, as Christ also hath loved us,
and hath given himself for us an offering and a sacrifice
to God for a sweetsmelling savour." (Ephesians 5:2)

A Husband is a Gardener

A husband is a gardener and his wife is a garden. If he fails to take care of his garden, weeds of sarcasm, anger, bitterness, boredom, and resentment will start to grow. It is at this point that every man has one of three choices:

1. The husband can choose to change gardens by way of leaving his spouse.

Although it is an unscriptural choice, if a man wants to, he can choose to leave his wife. It is not what he signed up for, nor would this choice correlate with the covenant of marriage. But, if providence chooses to leave him to his own devices, he can walk away from his marriage.

2. The husband can keep his garden, yet grow bitter about the weeds.

I feel that most men in a less than perfect marriage fall underneath this present category. Instead of making the appropriate changes in their lives, they will stay in the marriage, yet get bitter about the negative aspects of their wife, and the relationship in general. Colossians 3:19 admonishes:

> *"Husbands, love your wives,*
> *and be not bitter against them."*

The Lord gives this command because he is more than aware that a man's temptation is to live selfishly, yet complain about the byproduct of living in such a manner. His primary weakness is to become disgusted with the very weeds that his lack of care has allowed to grow.

3.   The husband can start doing what it takes to prevent the weeds from growing in his garden.

Option number three is not only best, but scriptural, and it involves the husband serving his wife as he would his own interests and desires. (Ephesians 5:28) Of course, as mentioned in the last point, he can choose to complain about the weeds, but that will do little to further the cause of happiness in his marriage. He will do more to endear success by taking sole responsibility for the state of his garden and serve his wife as he agreed to do when he made a covenant before God and others.

I find that many men are short sighted in that they fail to see that their actions have exposed their wives to their emotional vulnerabilities. When they should have been focusing on the cause, they seem to become embittered about the effect. A failure to reverse this order will be the source of little or no progress in a man's marriage. It will only serve as an impetus for a lukewarm relationship at best.

I have also seen that men will do more to fast-forward the problem-solving process if they will ask themselves questions as such: If I had been sacrificially loving my wife from day one of our marriage, would she have ever felt so tempted to act in a negative manner to my behavior? Or, if I had been properly taking care of my garden in the first place, would these weeds of anger, sarcasm, unforgiveness, and resentment even be growing?

Bank Account

A woman is like a bank account in that a man can only withdraw what is first being deposited through unconditional love and kindness.

If any of us withdraw more than we deposit at a real banking institution, we will soon receive a statement from the bank telling us of our error. The same is true in marriage, yet I have found that the banks are usually a lot nicer in the way that they give their statements than most of our wives.

When a man sees that his wife is delivering negative statements, he has three similar choices to that of the gardener. He can either change banks (this is not scriptural), argue with the statements and deny their veracity, or he can start making the appropriate deposits.

Men will find it a far better option to start making reasonable deposits by loving and serving their wives. Other approaches have been tried, but all have failed.

Queen of Sheba

Upon first meeting their wives, men are superb about treating them like the Queen of Sheba. At this juncture, women feel they are in their rightful place as they have a sense of feeling valued, protected, and secure about the relationship. Be that as it may, through time and circumstance, some of these very same women slowly become dethroned from the royal palace only to be replaced by their husband's job, career, business endeavors, hobbies, or feelings of boredom and familiarity. As a result, disillusionment follows, and many women are tempted to act in a way that is less than becoming.

For the average husband, the solution to what seems to be complex marriage problems is often simple, and it usually involves putting his wife back in her rightful place in the royal palace. If there is a failure in this area, the little girl within her that longs to feel beautiful and cherished will be tempted to deem herself second rate. Outwardly she will still look pretty. But, inwardly she will fight against the mixed messages that resound from her husband's actions as they will cause her to feel devalued at best.

Deep down, wives want to know that their husband's business endeavors and hobbies are not his mistress. It is not so much that she desires to win out among these, as much as she despises the very thought of even having to compete against them.

I like to tell men that to make headway in their marriage, they must do now for love's sake what they did before marriage for self's sake. In other words, when couples first exchange their "I love yous," they really mean, "I love what you are doing for me," or "I love the way you make me feel." Now, despite their potentially despondent feelings, we encourage men to serve their wives as they did when they first met, yet with a motive of true, sacrificial love.

I am a firm believer that if some men treated their wives on the first, second, and third date as they have in the last few years, there would never have been a fourth, fifth, or sixth date. Interestingly enough, without marriage speakers, counselors, and marriage conferences, men know how to gain the heart of their wives before marriage. Now, some play dumb while others choose ignorance. I say, if you knew how to get her to sign on the dotted line to begin with, for the most part, you can probably figure out how to keep her around.

Wife Training

Husbands are better than they realize at training their wives. However, this training is of a different sort as it takes little or no effort to accomplish.

When I was young, my mother would ask me to clean my room, take out the trash, or go outside and feed the dogs. To my shame, I would often ignore her requests until, finally, she would lose her cool for the purpose of gaining my attention. Without knowing it, I was subtly training my mother that she had to use anger to control my actions.

Similarly, when I was first married, I would not change my behavior or show concern toward my wife until she was either in tears or outwardly displaying her frustrations. In an odd sort of way, I was training her that to get me motivated she had to use either anger or some other form of drastic behavior.

Many wives do not want to show anger or hostility toward their husbands. It is just that from their viewpoint, anger works to get their husbands motivated to take decisive action.

If you are a man that is married to an incessantly angry or frustrated woman, you may want to consider that it is entirely possible that through your laziness or lack of cognizance you have left her with few options. In her mind, the last and only resort may be to nag, harp, or lose her cool.

Wilted Flower

Early in our marriage, my wife was like a wilted flower. I had sucked the life right out of her through my temper tantrums, late night lectures, and inconsistent behavior. To make matters worse, I was an assistant pastor of a church, therefore, I had a verse for everything. In fact, once she said, "You have a verse for everything you say." I quickly retorted by saying, "Well, the Bible says to 'let every man be fully persuaded.'"

Seeing that Melody's spirit was closed to me, I quickly became defensive in my spirit. Not enjoying the emotional distance between us, I would try to breach the gap between our hearts by managing her thoughts and emotions through carefully constructed arguments and pleas. To be honest, it only made matters worse.

At one point, I was convinced that God had given me the wrong person. I was adamant that she was either rebellious in heart or simply closed-minded toward biblical truth about marriage. The only thing I had not considered was that I was responsible for the dry condition of my flower.

Not too long into the marriage, something happened. I vividly remember the day when the Lord showed me that I had been the problem, as I was not pouring on her the sunlight, water, and nutrients of unconditional love and kindness. As I took personal responsibility for the state of my flower and started taking care of her as God would have me to, something even better happened. All of the things that I had tried to get out of her by using anger, guilt, and pressure, I started to receive from her as a result of loving her unconditionally. The truth is, once I began taking care of my flower in a biblical way, her petals came back to life and she opened her heart to me as she had once done when we initially met.

Thought-Provoking Questions:

1. What is the first step for the men in our 2-step process?

2. Would you agree that if the average man were to treat his business clients and associates as he does his wife, he would probably be broke or out of a job a long time ago?

3. Do you treat those closest to you, the worst or the best?

4. Would your spouse and children agree with your answer to the last question?

5. What is the fundamental problem between husbands and wives as related in this chapter? (Ephesians 5:28)

6. In relation to the gardener illustration, what are the three choices that a husband has in a troubled marriage?

7. At times, a husband will fail to take care of his wife, and then complain about the weeds of anger, sarcasm, and resentment that grow in her heart. Have you been guilty of this? (Colossians 3:19)

8. In relation to our banking illustration, do your deposits cover the amount of withdrawals in your marriage?

9. Is your wife sending out statements to you that you are withdrawing from her emotional bank account more than you are depositing?

10. Did you treat your wife like the Queen of Sheba before marriage?

11. Has she slowly become dethroned from the royal palace?

12. If so, what has replaced her on that throne?

13. Does your wife feel that she has to use negativity in order to motivate you to take decisive action?

14. Does your wife have wilted petals? Will reasoning with her help to bring life back to these petals?

15. What are some ways that you can start to treat your wife like a world-class business client?

16. What can you do now for love's sake that you did before marriage for self's sake?

Closing Prayer:

Lord, help the husbands in our audience to treat
those closest to them the best, especially their wives.
Give then a love for their wives that mirrors
Christ love for the church.

Chapter 9

THE FIRST STEP
FOR THE WOMEN

For men, romance starts in the eyes and then has a way of moving to the rest of the body. For women, things are a little different, as romance starts in the realm of their imagination.

Even at an early age, women start to get an idea of what they want their man, their marriage, and, consequently, their life to be. When these fail to measure up to their expectations, women are tempted to make what I call the mistake of mistakes, by becoming negative in the way they approach their husbands.

Most women do not marry the man they have, as much as the man they want or expect him to be. When these two fail to agree, many of these very same women are tempted to try to bring about change or defend their cause by picking up what I call the sword of negativity.

The first step for women is simple: lay down your swords of anger, resentment, coldness, apathy, or hostility and start using biblical weaponry.

The Wise and the Foolish Woman

Women sometimes find lousy ways to promote change or defend themselves in a marriage. To tell the truth, some women are downright foolish in how they choose to fight for their marriage.

It is understood as to why some women feel hurt, betrayed, and devalued. But, in a difficult marriage, acting according to these very same feelings will only serve to drive away any hope of success.

Proverbs 14:1 says:

"Every wise woman buildeth her house: but the foolish plucketh it down with her hands."

The tricky aspect of applying this verse is that most women do not consciously set out to destroy their homes and act in a foolish manner. If the truth be told, very few women leave the wedding altar with a motive to make decisions that are detrimental to their marriage. But, I have found that where women err is not how they cause dysfunction, as much as how they react to it.

A woman's response to a dysfunctional man or marriage is usually the dividing line between a wise and a foolish woman. It is there that she will prove the depth of her wisdom or the lack thereof.

A foolish woman may be right in her assessment of her husband's faults and failures, but she is often unwise in how she responds to them. She fails to see that her negative reactions to his negative behavior are just as unbiblical and selfish in nature as his lack of love and affection toward her.

The scriptures indicate that we are just as responsible for how we react to the negative behavior of others as they are for instigating problems in the first place. This is evident in I Thessalonians 5:15, as Paul says:

> *"See that none render evil for evil unto any man;*
> *but ever follow that which is good, both among*
> *yourselves, and to all men."*

In I Peter 3:9, after Peter finished dealing with the subject of marriage, he states:

> *"Not rendering evil for evil, or railing for railing: but*
> *contrariwise blessing; knowing that ye are thereunto*
> *called, that ye should inherit a blessing."*

Martyrdom

A woman sometimes contributes to her own martyrdom by retreating behind a battle line of emotion and then tragically falling on her own sword of negativity. Oddly enough, she can often then be heard crying foul when her husband fails to come to her rescue.

Women become their own martyr by simply responding negatively toward their husband's faults and failures. With some, their resentment is painstakingly overt, while with others it is more subtle in nature. There are even those whose negativity is shrouded with a cloak of religion, in that they quote the sweet scriptures, yet with a spirit of bitterness.

Nonetheless, if a woman continues to respond to the negative behavior of her husband with a contentious spirit, she will eventually find herself injured by the very sword that she holds as a means of defense.

In my book on anger, Angry Without a Cause, I take the time to talk about the futility of a woman using anger to combat her husband's dysfunctional or unloving behavior. Here is an excerpt from chapter 2 of my book on anger:

> "The woman that ridicules her husband by making sarcastic remarks and subtle inferences to his lack of leadership and abilities is not only hurting her husband, but also herself. She is not only ensuring that he will have a tough time rising above her low view of him, but she will also end up despising him for not being half the man that she has discouraged him to be.
>
> Deep within, she will struggle with feelings of contempt, since she longs for a man to look up to, but not a man that will look down on her. The problem is that by displaying her inner frustrations toward him, she has become her own archenemy. With her cross looks and her deep sighs, she helps to dig a pit for him that will eventually cause her to become more and more disgusted at his lack of ability to crawl out of it."

Additionally, the wife whose actions and words are minced with negativity may find her husband too weak or tired to push through the emotional battle lines she has erected.

I will be the first to agree that men should show themselves valiant enough to deal with the battle scene in question. There is no doubt that men should be willing to push through those battle lines of emotion with unwavering determination as they wield their swords of unconditional love and kindness. But, if I may, a woman has an ability to build a mighty strong battle line of emotion that seems almost impenetrable at times. And, instead of crying foul that the man has not the strength nor the determination to push through, she may find it better to lay down her swords of negativity and allow that battle line of emotion to fall down flat.

Wedding Vows Revisited

In our Christian anger management book, I wrote:

"Throughout time, women have been tempted to withhold their love and affection toward their husbands because they fail to measure up to their expectations. A woman that has given in to this temptation must realize that when she holds back from loving her husband because he doesn't meet her standards, she is simply holding her love as a ransom until he comes up with the appropriate payment. This is actually a form of manipulation. It is not what she signed up for when she said, 'I do.'"

A few chapters ago, we took the time to have a mock wedding ceremony. I would like to revisit that ceremony and enlarge upon it.

The first time, I asked you to imagine both saying, "I will love, honor, and cherish you as long as I feel like it." This time, I have a different hypothetical, but only for the bride. It is as such:

> "I will love, honor, and cherish you as long as you measure up to my expectations."

Could you imagine the thoughts of the witnesses? As they make eyes at one another, they would be thinking, "This one is never going to last."

The illustration is almost comical, but it is a reality in many, if not most, marriages today. This is because when a man fails to measure up to the expectations of his wife, her first temptation is either to express her disappointment or suppress her love toward him. The problem is that she did not covenant to love him in such a way. She signed up to love the man she has, not the man she supposed him to be, and, unfortunately, there is sometimes a great divide between the two.

Biblical Weaponry

There are three swords that I urge women to pick up as they set down the swords of anger, coldness, or resentment. These are the swords of thankfulness, gentleness, and faith. First of all, we will consider the sword of thankfulness.

The Sword of Thankfulness

I truly believe that if you go back to the Garden of Eden, you can learn just about everything you need to know about mankind. In the Genesis story, we find these details in Genesis 3:1-7:

> *"Now the serpent was more subtle than any beast of the field which the Lord God had made. And he said unto the woman, Yea, hath God said, Ye shall not eat of every tree of the garden?*
>
> *And the woman said unto the serpent, We may eat of the fruit of the trees of the garden: But of the fruit of the tree which is in the midst of the garden, God hath said, Ye shall not eat of it, neither shall ye touch it, lest ye die.*
>
> *And the serpent said unto the woman, Ye shall not surely die: For God doth know that in the day ye eat thereof, then your eyes shall be opened, and ye shall be as gods, knowing good and evil.*
>
> *And when the woman saw that the tree was good for food, and that it was pleasant to the eyes, and a tree to be desired to make one wise, she took of the fruit thereof, and did eat, and gave also unto her husband with her; and he did eat.*
>
> *And the eyes of them both were opened, and they knew that they were naked; and they sewed fig leaves together, and made themselves aprons."*

Obviously, both Adam and Eve were in the wrong, but it is interesting to see that the serpent tempted Eve with a desire to have more than she already had. Though it is never wrong to want more love and closeness in your marriage, I do feel there is a great lesson here to be learned: it was being unthankful for what Eve had that caused her to touch the forbidden fruit.

I often counsel that if you know what threw you into your mess, you can often find how to get out. According to Genesis, discontentment was Eve's greatest temptation. It was the catalyst that caused her disobedience.

A wife will do well to understand that Eve's struggle may very well be hers. And, if Eve in her perfection was grappling with being unthankful, how much more will women with wayward flesh and an imperfect husband do the same? This may be part of the reason why Paul said in I Corinthians 7:28 that "if thou marry . . . such shall have trouble in the flesh."

For the women, taking hold of the sword of thankfulness involves finding the good in their husbands and offering them praise as a result of what they find. Before moving on, I would like to consider a few vital points about this part of the first step:

1. The scriptures command us to have a thankful spirit:

In pastoral counseling sessions, life coaching sessions, and marriage conferences, I have found the use of Philippians 4:8 to be a very powerful verse. It states:

> *"Finally, brethren, whatsoever things are true,*
> *whatsoever things are honest, whatsoever things are just,*
> *whatsoever things are pure, whatsoever things are lovely,*
> *whatsoever things are of good report; if there be any*
> *virtue, and if there be any praise, think on these things."*

Paul is teaching us to dwell on whatever we can find that is positive in any situation. This would have to also include our own marriages and even a less than perfect husband.

In I Thessalonians 5:18, Paul also said:

> *"In every thing give thanks: for this is the will of God*
> *in Christ Jesus concerning you."*

If you will notice, Paul did not suggest these things as much as they are commanded.

2.   There is always something to be thankful for.

Whether a man is always in a rush, disorganized, absent-minded, aloof, unhelpful with the kids, or too critical, there is usually some way to walk in obedience to Philippians 4:8.

A man may continually come home late from work, but the wise woman will take the time to, at the very least, thank him for working so hard for the family. A husband might be irresponsible in the way he handles money or lazy when it comes to household chores, but the more effective approach will be to praise him into a better man than to berate him into a worse.

3. An unthankful heart is a deep chasm.

It has been said, "To whom enough is not plenty, plenty will never be enough." In like manner, I like to counsel that an unthankful heart in anyone is like a bottomless pit that can never be filled.

Some wives have passed up a number of good men in search of a storybook man or marriage. This is usually a problem as they are often chasing a mirage or something that only exists on a television screen or in a fiction book.

Not one of us married someone as perfect as Christ. That is a good thing, by the way, because if our spouses were as perfect as Christ, they probably would not have picked us as a mate in the first place.

In any case, thankfulness in a woman's heart is key, as some men feel that no matter what they do or say, it is to no avail. From their perspective, they might as well be filling a bag full of holes because the reality of who they are always seems to come short of the fantasy of what their wives want them to become.

Thankfulness in a wife has a way of filling the holes in the bag mentioned above, or giving a bottom to that bottomless pit. It replaces a mirage with a realistic goal, and it gives the man a little more encouragement to exhibit love even in the presence of his imperfections.

4. A thankful spirit will help to promote an atmosphere where change has a greater chance of happening.

When a woman reacts to the negative behavior of her husband by acting cold, indifferent, sarcastic, rude, emotionally or physically absent in bed, or outright angry, her husband will seldom feel like mending his ways. If anything, he will either meet her with the same amount of anger, or the more passive man will retreat into his emotional or physical cave.

In a troubled marriage, it is vital that a woman learn to control what she is able to control. Many call it controlling that which is controllable. If this does not occur, then a woman will feel powerless and, therefore, enslaved to the negative behavior of her husband.

When a woman chooses to wield the biblical sword of thankfulness, she is helping herself to gain some sense of control in her marriage. As she looks for the good and responds accordingly, she is helping to promote a climate where change has a better chance of taking place. Instead of sulking, pouting, or complaining to others about her plight, she is showing herself to be more than a victim. She is a warrior that is fighting a battle in which the outcome is not based upon her husband's inconsistencies, but in the Providence of the Almighty God.

The Sword of Gentleness

If, as a woman, you are going to plead for God's help for your marriage, then you should also understand the importance of walking in His precepts.

In I John 3:22-23, the Bible says:

"And whatsoever we ask, we receive of him, because we keep his commandments, and do those things that are pleasing in his sight. And this is his commandment, That we should believe on the name of his Son Jesus Christ, and love one another, as he gave us commandment."

John tells us that if we are going to call upon the Lord for help, then we should also be careful to walk in His ways. Clearly, it is not enough to say, "God bless me." It is also of utmost importance that we be in a what I call a bless-able position.

All that being said, I have found that men and women alike have a propensity to claim the promises of God concerning their marriage yet neglect His commands when it comes to dealing with their spouse. The two must go hand in hand. In reality, we might as well be holding a lucky charm or clinging to a rabbit's foot if we are going to have such an approach. (Proverbs 28:9)

At any rate, if a woman in a difficult marriage wants to abide in a bless-able position, she should understand the necessity of utilizing biblical weaponry. One of those weapons, the sword of thankfulness, has already been mentioned. The second is the sword of gentleness.

Contrary to popular opinion, nice guys do not finish last. In fact, the scriptures teach the exact opposite. Proverbs 25:15 says:

"By long forbearing is a prince persuaded, and a soft tongue breaketh the bone."

To be honest, this is one of those scriptures that you tend to pass over as you read through the book of Proverbs. Its meaning seems slightly obscure at the onset, but a closer look will reveal a very powerful truth.

Proverbs 25:15 tells us that a "soft tongue" is a powerful weapon. It teaches us that if you are trying to break a bone of disunity and dysfunction, softness mixed with patience should be a person's first choice.

There is an old Chinese proverb which states that he who strikes the first blow admits he has lost. This is accurate in that when a person loses their cool, they are usually giving off the message that they have little substance behind their argument. In a not so subtle fashion, they are conveying the message that their anger is the last leg upon which they are standing.

Proverbs 16:32 admonishes:

"He that is slow to anger is better than the mighty; and
he that ruleth his spirit than he that taketh a city."

Solomon is teaching us that a calm spirit breeds strength rather than weakness. If you think about it, when others around you lose their temper, they also usually lose the ability to influence others for good. What they gain in satisfaction, they lose in credibility.

When I counsel spouses that are dealing with hard hearts and stubborn attitudes, I typically recommend that they, first of all, do everything they can to disarm their situation with a spirit of gentleness. Ephesians 4:32 states:

"And be ye kind one to another, tenderhearted, forgiving one another, even as God for Christ's sake hath forgiven you."

Notice the use of the word "tenderhearted" in this verse. Paul is teaching us that we are not only to concentrate on what we do for others, but also the spirit in which those things are done.

I have found that it is hard for a person to fight with someone that refuses to fight back. It is also doubly difficult to be mad at someone that responds in a gentle fashion.

Of course, there are times when tough love must be shown, and there are definitely instances when a woman must show love by flexing her spiritual and emotional muscles. There are also times when a woman should make moves to protect herself if her well being is in danger.

But, if you are dealing with what some would call normal marital conflict, you may want to give heed to not only what you are doing but how you are doing it. Instead of simply focusing on what you are saying, you may want to consider the spirit in which your words are spoken.

If I served two cups of coffee, one may be boiling hot while the other is just right to the taste. Which one would most people prefer? Although both are filled with coffee, most would probably pass over the one that is seething hot.

In like manner, couples having issues often exchange words that seem harmless, yet they are said in a way that is less than edifying. Though their words appear innocent, they are sometimes seething with a harsh or a critical spirit.

Even when husbands and wives in a difficult marriage say, "Don't forget to pick up the kids," or "Hand me the phone," they often send out another message. They are, many times, saying the same words as they did in a better time of their marriage, yet in a way that is condescending at best.

Softening your spirit will require you to watch your tone of voice and approach your husband in a kind and affectionate manner. It means that instead of saying, "Where are the keys to the car?" in a cutting way, as if he is purposefully hiding them, you say the same words, yet with an entirely different spirit. Rather than saying hello on the phone, as if your husband is a bill collector, greet him in a warm and congenial fashion.

I know that upon reading this some will affirm, "I have tried being nice." However, think about this: have you tried being nice in your spirit?

Keep in mind, people are spiritual beings deep down inside. Therefore, if you want to really affect a person, you must reach their spirit.

People do not simply observe with their eyes and listen with their ears. Their spirit is discerning your spirit, and if you want another's spirit to open to you, then you will find it vital to approach them with a spirit of gentleness.

Before moving on, start asking yourself the following questions about the way you have been dealing with your husband:

1. Have I been kind and tenderhearted in the way I have been speaking to him?

2. Are my words minced with a cold or a critical spirit?

3. Is my tone of voice or the spirit in which I talk mingled with sarcasm or disrespect?

4. Is the spirit in which I speak and act when dealing with my husband in line with Ephesians 4:32?

The Sword of Faith

As a woman learns to lay down the sword of negativity, I would also recommend that, in its place, she grasp the sword of faith. Here are a few ways in which I would suggest the accomplishing of this task:

1. A wife could begin to look at her husband in a different light.

I Corinthians 13:7 tells us that charity or true love "believeth all things" and "hopeth all things." Quite frankly, this verse is teaching us that in order to love an unlovable person, we must learn to look beyond what we have ever known about them and toward what they can become through Divine intervention.

When applied to marriage, I Corinthians 13:7 is a powerful verse as it invokes a woman to look at something else besides her husband's past and present failures. According to the verse, biblical love will cause her to look more at the potential that he has in Christ.

In Judges 6-8, the scriptures provide for us a story about a man called Gideon. You may remember him as a great warrior and a courageous leader, but that is only because we tend to focus on the story's ending.

There was a time when Gideon seemed to fall short of exhibiting a hero's demeanor. In verse 11 of Judges 6, the Bible gives us a look at another side of Gideon:

> *"And there came an angel of the Lord, and sat under an oak which was in Ophrah, that pertained unto Joash the Abiezrite: and his son Gideon threshed wheat by the winepress, to hide it from the Midianites."*

This verse has always intrigued me in that we do not see Gideon as the fearless leader that led 300 men against an army of over 135,000 soldiers. Instead, we see him as a man living in subjection to not only the Midianites, but also his fears and inhibitions.

In verse 15 of the same chapter, we find him saying this in response to the angel of the Lord:

> *"And he said unto him, Oh my Lord, wherewith shall I save Israel? behold, my family is poor in Manasseh, and I am the least in my father's house."*

Once again, this is hardly the talk of a leader full of faith and courage. It is the verbiage of a man with a defeatist mindset.

Nonetheless, in these passages of scripture, we find Gideon having an encounter with a messenger from Heaven. Carefully look at the salutation of the angel of the Lord in Judges 6:12, as it gives us a glimpse of Heaven's view of Gideon:

> *"And the angel of the Lord appeared unto him, and said unto him, The Lord is with thee, thou mighty man of valour."*

I have often been enamored with the angel's greeting to Gideon as it seems to go directly against human nature. Think about it. How do we see Gideon with the evidence supplied in the book of Judges? Frankly, we see him as impoverished, insecure, and a subject to the tyrannical rule of the Midianites. On the other hand, even though Heaven sees the same, the angel looks past the obvious and into the future as he calls him a "mighty man of valour."

I believe that many wives can learn a great lesson from the angel, in that dwelling on the obvious rarely works to help their cause. To be honest, in the long run, it does more harm than good, and a wife will probably do more to extract greatness out of her husband by practicing "I Corinthians 13 love," rather than what comes naturally.

Before moving on, I would like to point out that this little bit of advice is not some magic potion that guarantees that your husband will eventually change. There are times when a man stays as he is. Yet, I have found that this step is not as much for the man as it is for the woman.

It has a way of positively affecting her overall attitude and feelings, which will find a way of coming to the surface through her words, tone of voice, and facial expressions.

2. A wife could have faith that she will eventually feel differently about her husband.

Though we have already discussed the danger of following your emotions, I am a firm believer that emotions are not necessarily evil in and of themselves. In fact, at some point, God desires your emotions, principles, and actions to be going in the same direction that the Holy Spirit is leading you. Once this occurs, I believe you have a winning combination.

Nevertheless, at this time, you may have very few feelings for your husband. If you find yourself in this position, I have found it vital that women learn to have faith that if they change their behavior toward their husband, their feelings will frequently follow suit.

I have often encouraged women to apply this principle in a very practical way by having them ask themselves this question: If I truly felt love for my husband today, how would I be acting? Then, I advise women to go and do according to their answer. To be honest, it is a powerful step for women to take, and there is a sense where it must be done in faith that their feelings will eventually agree with not only their actions, but biblical precepts.

Thought Provoking Questions:

1. What are your thoughts on the statement: "Most women do not marry the man they have, as much as the man they want him to be"?

2. Have you been tempted to take hold of the sword of negativity in order to defend your cause or bring about change in your marriage?

3. What is the first step for the women in our 2-step process?

4. What are some swords that you may need to lay down?

5. What are some ways that you have chosen to fight for your marriage that have done more to harm your marriage than to help it?

6. What are the three biblical swords that are recommended to use, instead of the sword of negativity?

7. I gave four reasons as to why wives should utilize the sword of thankfulness. Can you name two of them?

8. What are some ways that you can start using the sword of thankfulness in your marriage? (Philippians 4:8)

9. Do nice guys finish last? Do your actions show that you agree or disagree with your answer?

10. What does the Bible teach us in Proverbs 25:15? Is your spirit soft or hardened toward your husband? (Ephesians 4:32)

11. What are some ways you can take hold of the sword of faith?

12. Do you look at your husband for what he has been, or for what he could become, by God's grace?

13. If you felt love for your husband today, what would you be doing differently than what you are already doing?

Closing Prayer:

Lord, help the wives in our audience to lay down weaponry that is not only unblibcal in nature, but harmful to their marriages. Help them to have the proper balance between unconditonal love and tough love.

Chapter 10

THE SECOND STEP

The second step of our 2-step process is the same for both the men and the women. Quite simply, it is to study your spouse and act accordingly.

I Peter 3:7 instructs husbands to dwell with their wives "according to knowledge." The meaning of this phrase seems to be fairly obvious in that husbands are to acquaint themselves with the needs of their wives. We have taken this verse in part and applied it to both the husband and the wife in that we encourage both to familiarize themselves with the needs of the other.

Our second step has two distinct parts. They are as such:

1. Acknowledge and appreciate the differences between you and your spouse.

2. Take interest in the interests of the other.

Acknowledging and Appreciating the Differences

Either God had a sense of humor when he created marriage or He had our best interest in mind. I choose to believe the latter, although, at times, I have toyed with the former.

It is true. Opposites attract. This is why I commonly assert that husbands and wives are two very different looking pieces of the same two-piece puzzle. When they fit together in love, they paint a beautiful picture of the glory of God and Christ's love for the church.

I sometimes detect that many view the differences between men and women as a handicap to having a healthy relationship. I take exception with that approach in that it is entirely probable that the differences are not designed to be stumbling blocks as much as stepping stones to a God-glorifying, divorce-defying marriage.

When a relationship is functioning as it should, the differences between a husband and a wife prove to be helpful in a multitude of areas. Here are four, just to name a few:

1. The differences between a man and a woman help to promote balance in a relationship.

Imagine trying to steady a see-saw all by yourself. It is possible, yet it is more difficult than having one person at each end. In the same way, the differences between many husbands and wives, in a more functional relationship, serve to promote a healthy balance that positively affects every area of their lives.

2. The differences allow each individual in the marriage to be themselves.

Have you ever noticed that people that are just alike often do not get along that well? Instead of meshing together they are often competing against each other to be themselves.

If two talkers are married to one another, who would be listening? If a pair of romantics are joined in union, who would there be to woo, if both are in hot pursuit of one another all the time?

3. Differences in a marriage help to provide an opportunity for a healthy form of tension in a relationship.

Tension in the strings of a violin is what allows the instrument to play beautiful music. It also serves to ignite sporting competitions and, during times of war, it keeps soldiers on high alert.

In the same way, the tension that comes from two opposites having to exercise great care to meet the other person's needs can provide an edge to a relationship that would be nonexistent if both were exactly alike.

4. The differences between a man and his wife greater enhance the potential for more energy in the relationship.

Cold and warm air create an atmosphere that welcomes tornado-like activity. Unfortunately, the same seems to occur in dysfunctional marriages in that the differences between both parties sometimes creates an energy that leaves a path of destruction.

Conversely, for electricity to flow, both positive and negative electrons are required. When correctly harnessed, electricity proves to be wildly beneficial.

Like electricity, the differences between a man and a woman produce an energy that has the potential to be used for good. Without these differences, the husband and wife would probably notice a diminished level of excitement in their relationship.

Opposites Attract, but Eventually Repel

What attracts you to someone has a way of repelling you from them at a later time. This is true for all relationships, especially marriage.

Upon first meeting my wife, I noticed she possessed an inner strength that was very appealing to me. Believe it or not, after having a mere 20 minute conversation with her, I commented to one of my college mates, "I think I am going to be in a long-lasting relationship with that girl, if not marriage." My intuition proved to be accurate as we have recently celebrated twenty years of matrimony.

Not too long after returning from our honeymoon, I noticed that my wife's strong and slightly stoic demeanor was not as attractive as I once perceived it to be. This was because, when we had a spat, I found that it had a way of inhibiting my childish behavior, and the boyish side of me was taken aback.

Melody is not an extremely verbal person. I appreciated this when we first met, as I noticed I rarely had to compete for floor time during our conversations.

Be that as it may, a few years into marriage, I remember complaining that it was a rarity for my wife to freely offer compliments. I also recall pointing out that her apologies were few and far between. Interestingly enough, though my concern was over her lack of verbosity, in the very beginning of our relationship, I saw this is as a plus.

I have an intense personality, and I do not like to take no for an answer. My wife, on the other hand, is different in that she is a little more laid back.

From the early days of our relationship, Melody has respected my persistence in accomplishing what I set my mind to do, and she has always excelled at throwing her support my way. The only problem is that, over the years, my persistence has spilled over into other areas of my life, such as the marriage bed, and silly discussions about where to eat and what to do during recreational activities.

Sometimes, my tenacity can be a little overwhelming to my wife, and, to be frank, it has probably been the cause of most of our disagreements. Nevertheless, it intrigues me to see that what was probably the greatest attractant for my wife also turned out to be a hindrance of sorts in our relationship.

It is true that opposites attract, but as you can see, what attracts couples to one another has a way of repelling them from each other at a later time.

The Snow Versus the Cold

When speaking on marriage, I share what seems to be a rather obscure expression regarding the differences between husbands and wives. Though its meaning may be elusive at first, most find it to be extremely beneficial as they discover its sense.

I often point out:

> It is hypocritical to play in the snow of your spouse's oppositeness five days out of the week, yet complain about the cold that comes with it on the sixth day.

In other words, it is a double standard to enjoy the benefits of your spouse's oppositeness on one day, yet become critical or argumentative when you perceive that same attribute to be working against you on another day.

I have already mentioned that my wife, Melody, has a deep inner strength. Along with that, she is not loud, nor is she very flamboyant. She is what I call a "stable-Mable."

I, on the other hand, am her exact opposite in that I am not a "steady-Eddie." I can be up one day and feeling a little down the next.

Honestly, I have played in the snow of my wife being an emotionally stable person for many years in that she has served as an emotional anchor in our home. I may go up and down, but she is usually very even-keeled. In fact, we have a little saying around the home that states that mom is not allowed to have a bad day. The rest of us may be all over the place, but the case must not be so with Mother.

For years, Melody has helped to keep my feet on the ground and my head above the emotional waters, by her mere steadfastness. I have, indeed, played heartily in that snow.

One the other hand, every now and then, I start to feel the cold that has a way of accompanying that snow. That is, sometimes, I have big plans and wishes that I verbalize to my wife. It may be concerning business, the church, or pleasurable activities, and I usually come to her anticipating that she will be just as excited as I am. The only problem, if you wish to call that, is that "stable-Mables" do not do back flips upon hearing about new ideas and endeavors. Normally, they ponder them in their hearts for long periods of time before making any decisions or throwing their support toward a cause.

It is at this time that conflict could ensue for my wife and me. This is because although I have been playing in the snow of her steadfastness for most of my marriage, at this point, I could easily start to feel the cold that sometimes accompanies the snow of her being a "stable-Mable."

In the early days of our marriage, I would share new ideas with Melody with the expectation that she would jump on board with reckless abandon upon hearing my grand ideas. To my chagrin, I would be met with kind nods and thoughtful expressions, but not the emotion that I desired. It was not too long into those conversations that I would start to accuse my wife of lacking faith and vision for the future. I would be sure to relate to her that successful people have to constantly be looking for new mountains to climb and sitting back and doing nothing would do little to move us forward.

Looking back, I can see that my wife did not lack faith, vision, or an ability to be forward thinking. She simply had a different way of processing new ideas, and her approach was not necessarily bad. It was just different.

As you can see, I had a problem in the area of thankfulness. What I needed to do was to catch myself and say something within, like, "It is hypocritical to go negative on my wife because she is not falling down in awe of my new ideas. From an emotional level, she is very steady, and I have benefited from this in many ways throughout my marriage. Right now, I need to accept that this is all part of the package of being married to someone that is not as prone to emotional highs and lows as myself."

Melody is a natural saver. I am a natural spender. Believe me when I say that I have played in the snow of her being a saver for years.

Some years ago, we planted a new church in Pennsylvania. During that time, we lived on love because there was scarcely anything but love in our home.

Needless to say, during that time, I played in the snow of my wife being a saver in that she is the queen of frugality. I do not know how she does it, but she is one of those women that has a knack for taking ten cents and turning it into ten dollars.

My wife shops at yard sales, buys in bulk, and has mastered the art of couponing. Her middle name is Beth, but I think it could be Bargain.

Once again, I have played in the snow of Melody's oppositeness for years, yet there are times when the spender in me on a Friday evening jumps to my feet and says, "Let's all go out and get some hot chocolate!"

As all the children run to their rooms to find their shoes while singing my praises, the saver in my wife starts to come out as she calculates the cost. It is at that point that the saver and the spender could start to butt heads if care is not taken.

This is the point where arguments start for many couples. But, I have found that a simple attitude of gratitude goes a long way in these situations. (Philippians 4:8)

In my case, it is unbelievably helpful and calming to say within myself, "I have played in the snow of Melody's frugality for years. If I start to get snippy or tense, then it is hypocritical for me to enjoy the benefits of her frugality for most of the week and then become childish in my behavior when I perceive that I am not getting what I want."

A Little Check in Your Spirit Will do Wonders

A little check in your spirit before displaying any type of animosity toward your spouse will help you to avoid many spats. For some reason, this little step has a way of keeping anger at bay, and I find that it helps couples to avoid 75 to 80 percent of their previous arguments.

I am a problem solver. By itself, it is a tremendous quality to possess, as it helps me to be extremely focused when counseling, coaching, and rebuilding things that are falling apart.

Notwithstanding, the trouble is that problem solvers tend to be critically minded. As a matter of fact, if you were to show me a wall that you painted, I would be inclined to notice the one place where you missed a spot or had a run.

For years, Melody has played in the snow of my problem solving abilities in that it has allowed me to make a living for the family. As a pastor, church planter, life coach, and a speaker on issues of vital importance, I utilize my problem solving abilities on a daily basis. The only trouble is that there is a cold that comes with this snow. That is, there are times when I over-analyze my family, or try to solve too many problems around the home, rather than overlooking issues that are of less importance.

During some of these moments, it is helpful for my wife to remember that before she confronts my imbalance, she should be thankful for the snow that accompanies this cold. In other words, it helps to keep a spirit of anger and frustration in check when she says to herself, "Most of the time, I play in the snow of his problem solving abilities, and, though I will address this issue, I will be calm, as it is hypocritical of me not to accept that this is the cold that accompanies this snow."

Of course, this principle does not negate the fact that some issues need to be addressed. It would be absurd to assert that. But, I do find that acknowledging and appreciating the snow that accompanies the cold helps to keep couples calm when dealing with one another. It seems like such a small tweak, but I am finding this step to be ever so powerful for couples in need.

The Opposite Exercise

At our marriage conferences or pastoral care counseling sessions, I typically conduct what I call an opposite exercise. To be honest, I am not one for busy work, and I naturally despise rote learning as well as meaningless exercises. But, I have found that this simple little drill is very helpful to most couples. First, I recommend that you make a list of where you and your spouse are different from one another. I am not talking about one liking basketball versus football or Chinese food versus Italian, but differences such as these:

Organized - Messy

Outgoing - Introverted

Quiet - Talkative

Stationary - Risk taker

Big Picture Thinker - Detail Oriented

Skeptical - Accepting

Paranoid - Positive

Logical or Analytical - Emotional

Easy Going - Aggressive

Law - Grace

Spontaneous - Planner

Wait and See Attitude - Take Charge Attitude

Spender - Saver

Alert - Aloof

Passive - Domineering

Just to be clear, the proposed list of differences is not all inclusive. You may have a combination that is not necessarily listed. Nonetheless, start by coming up with three to four areas where you and your spouse are different.

After making the list, I would suggest that you look at the snow versus the cold. That is, make a few notes under each point that considers how your spouse's oppositeness works for you and how you perceive it to work against you. Although I have already given a few examples as to how to apply this, let me supply a few more. Keep in mind, these are simply examples. The details of your personal situation may be very different. I am simply providing a few ways to apply this so that you have a better understanding of how to carry out this exercise.

1. Organized versus messy

The cold for those married to messy or disorganized people:

> Messy or disorganized people tend to miss appointments, mismanage money, or are prone to be incessantly late. Their clutter can also be a point of derision, especially if they are married to a person with better organizational skills.

The snow associated with being married to someone that is messy:

> If your spouse is messy or disorganized, you are probably not thinking that your spouse's

disorganization could ever be of use. But, have you considered that your spouse's lack of organization gives place for your personal gifts to shine? Have you ever considered that you can often play the hero in the relationship because you are able to excel where they fall short?

Also, messy or disorganized people are sometimes very creative people. Though they do not excel at being organized, they often make up for this in that they are often artistic, musically inclined, or proficient at decorating. Focusing on these positives will probably help you to extract more greatness out of them than if you choose to be frustrated with them.

Conversely, the cold of being married to an organized person:

Heavily organized individuals are sometimes critical of those that do not measure up to their standards. This can pose a real problem for the person that is less organized, as they often feel they fall short of pleasing their spouse.

Also, organizers are often thrown off when things do not go according to plan. This can especially pose a problem if you are the more spontaneous one in the relationship. Your better half may often accuse you of sabotaging their system of doing things or ruining their plans.

The snow of being married to an organized person:

> People that are more organized often keep the ship afloat in that they make sure paperwork is filed, bills are paid, and important dates are on the calendar. Their giftedness in the area of organization often serves to keep day-to-day operations running smoothly.

2. Outgoing versus introverted

The cold for those married to an introvert or quiet person:

> Introverted or quiet people usually feel less of a need to share their feelings with their spouse. Consequently, they seldom seem to understand why the other person in the relationship would have such a need. This can be a difficult characteristic for a spouse that is more verbal in nature.

The snow associated with being married to someone that is either introverted or quiet:

> Quiet people tend to be more faithful, as they often have an ability to persevere while others tend to give up and quit.

> People that are more on the quiet side also have a knack of staying calm under pressure, whereas extroverts and talkative people often lose their cool in intense scenarios. This can be a very valuable asset to possess in many situations.

Conversely, the cold of being married to an outgoing person:

> Outgoing people are sometimes big talkers, yet they often fall short when it comes to carrying out what they have previously verbalized. This can be a frustrating part of being married to someone that is under such a category.

> Also, outgoing people are sometimes prone to lose their tempers faster. Whereas introverts tend to suppress their anger, outgoing people often express it by raising their voice, slamming things down, and reverting to name calling. This can all be very overwhelming to the person that is more on the quiet side.

The snow associated with being married to someone that is more outgoing:

> More often than not, outgoing people are fun to be around. What they lack in steadiness, they often make up in humor and whit.

> Also, the more introverted spouse can hide behind the social skills of the outgoing husband or wife at parties or social gatherings.

> Additionally, an outgoing personality may also help your spouse if they are involved in sales or a job that requires customer service skills.

3. Stationary versus risk taker

The cold of being married to a risk taker:

> Risk takers sometimes appear unstable to their spouses as they are often looking for new mountains to climb even when life seems to be going well.

> Also, because risk takers tend to be optimistic as well as entrepreneurial in spirit, they often rate a situation or opportunity by potential earnings and blessings. This usually poses a problem as they are typically married to someone that stays in the realm of the present when assessing their finances or life in general. This difference can serve as quite a dividing line between husbands and wives in such a state.

The snow of being married to a risk taker:

> Risk takers are often the life of the party. They can be fun, fly-by-the-seat-of-their-pants individuals that attract a lot of love and attention from others. One thing is for sure, living with a risk taker is never boring.

> As previously mentioned, risk takers are prone to be entrepreneurial in spirit. Though often on the edge of poverty, they do have the potential to earn a good deal of money if they ever find the right business plan and stick with it.

Conversely, the cold of being married to a stationary person:

> A stationary spouse can be frustrating to live with for their reluctance to step outside of their comfort zone and engage in what the risk taker would call an adventure.

The snow of being married to a stationary person:

> A stationary spouse is an anchor that holds a family on solid footing, even in difficult times.

4. Big picture thinker versus detail oriented

The cold of being married to a detail oriented person:

> Detail oriented people can appear to be more about the process rather than the results. This can frustrate a big picture thinker, as they feel the process is simply a means to an end, rather than the other way around. To a big picture thinker, details are a necessary evil, whereas, a detail oriented person may seem to have a different slant on the matter. This can cause quite the disturbance in marital unity.
>
> Also, when detail oriented people try to organize the people around them, resentment often occurs as others feel they are being treated as children.

The snow of being married to a detail oriented person:

> Detail oriented people are often good at paying the bills, organizing the house, and making sure important dates are on the calendar. Their contributions to the day to day operations of the household are usually extremely beneficial.

Conversely, the cold of being married to a big picture thinker:

> Big picture thinkers have difficulty focusing on details of the here and now. They may forget important dates and past events, leaving their spouse sometimes feeling unappreciated.

The snow of being married to a big picture thinker:

> The big picture thinker has a comforting handle on the future, and is adept at planning ahead, taking action before disasters strike, therefore giving the marriage security.

5. Skeptical versus accepting

The cold of being married to an accepting person:

> If you are married to a very accepting person, you probably feel they are taken advantage of from time to time. You have probably also used the word gullible to describe them on a number of occasions.

The snow of being married to an accepting person:

People that are more accepting of other people are often more easy-going, and they also have a gift for making people feel special. More prone to thankfulness, they have even used this gift to make their mate feel special.

I have also found that people that are more accepting of others seem to have a greater propensity to offer forgiveness.

Conversely, the cold of being married to a person that is skeptical:

People that are skeptical are often paranoid and are prone to complain. They can be difficult to be around as they seem to feed off of misery.

The snow of being married to a person that is skeptical:

People that are more skeptical in nature are often good problem solvers. This may help them to achieve a high level of success in their respective careers.

Additionally, people that have a skeptical mindset may be able to see evil where there is only a facade of good. They sometimes have a knack for discerning evil in a situation or a person before others are aware of such a problem.

6. Analytical versus emotional

The cold of being married to an emotional person:

> Black and white thinkers are often married to more
> emotional people. This can cause difficulties, as
> the more logical person in the relationship is often
> frustrated when the more emotional person has
> a difficult time seeing past their feelings. In their
> mind, logic trumps emotion at all times and in every
> situation. This usually causes issues when dealing
> with the children, purchasing houses and cars, and
> discerning between right and wrong.

The snow of being married to an emotional person:

> People that are more emotional bring an emotional
> spice to the home that black and white thinkers lack.
> Their emotions help to provide a warm spirit around
> the house that mere logic struggles to provide.

Conversely, the cold of being married to an analytical
person:

> Analytical spouses are sometimes perceived as cold
> and out of touch with the emotional needs of others
> in the home. They can also appear as lacking the
> grace needed to handle situations where feelings are
> involved.

The snow of being married to an analytical person:

Analytical people are often good to have around when it comes to solving problems, paperwork, crunching numbers, and figuring out technological issues. Even though one may feel that their black and white spouse is out of touch with the feelings of others in the home, there are probably a number of ways their natural bent is used for good.

The examples provided are simply a way to show you the possible ways that the opposite exercise can be applied. I typically find that spouses are far better at applying the snow versus cold principle to their marriage than I am.

After making your list of differences and jotting down the cold versus the snow, I would encourage you to talk about these with your spouse. If you have been guilty of taking your spouse for granted, acknowledge that and apologize for it.

Lastly, I would encourage you to take what you have learned from the exercise and catch yourself the next time you are about to exhibit your frustrations with your spouse. Start having that little check in your spirit that acknowledges the snow before you start to criticize the cold. You will find that it will have a way of tempering your harsh words and hurtful remarks.

Taking Interest in the Interests of Your Spouse

The second part of our second step involves taking interest in the interests of your spouse. Though this step may not be easy for some, I often say that if it was easy, then everyone would be doing it.

Properly loving your spouse will require you to do that which is not only illogical, but also least natural for you as a person. If you are newly married or in a premarital relationship, you may be hesitant to receive this adage. If you have been married for quite some time, I already have your ear.

Husbands and wives will do well to understand that they are not married to themselves. That is, their spouse has likes and dislikes that will seem almost nonsensical to them at times. All the same, in order to love one another in a way that takes hold, both will have to step outside of themselves and into the interests of the other.

Early in marriage, I thought Melody should consider herself to be the luckiest woman in the world. I was not trying to be egotistical as much as I had always heard that women craved affection, long conversations, and romance. To be honest, all of these came natural to me, therefore, I thought she would have it made. To my dismay, I found that my woman loved something of a different sort: dirt.

The last time Melody and I went house hunting, she looked to see if there was room for her garden and her chickens before even looking inside of the homes. This may sound a little funny to some, but you would have to know my wife to understand.

Not too long ago, my wife came home from shopping and began to tell me how she had splurged. For most women, that would mean a new dress, a day at the spa, or a fancy pedicure. Not so with Melody. That day she went all out and purchased a cultivator for her garden.

I, on the other hand, am not as impressed with soil, in that I am more of a romantic. I guess you could call me the "woman in the relationship" in that I am more about the date nights, the weekend escapes, and the frivolous purchases. In comparison to her, I could really care less about gardening and chickens, but there is one thing that I have to remember: I am not married to myself.

We once lived in a little blue house in Pennsylvania, and I learned that Melody wanted a garden. On my own accord, I went out and rented a rotor tiller and purchased about 200 lbs of sheep manure.

As I was working the fertilizer into her garden, she came out of the front door of our home glowing from head to toe. I remember thinking within myself, "I've tried flowers, date nights, chocolates, and jewelry, and sheep manure did the trick!"

As you can see, in order to love my wife in a way that affected her heart and opened her spirit, I had to come out of myself and step into her interests. Though it was illogical and contrary to my natural bent, it was, nonetheless, effective.

To this day, people see me on our little farm hauling mulch and picking up manure and are inclined to think that I love the outdoors. Not so much. What I enjoy more is having a happy wife.

Cornered

I am often cornered at social gatherings or in public places by those looking for advice. If I am exhausted from a hard week at work, I have found a way to shorten these conversations: I tell the truth.

On one such occasion, a young lady was bewailing her marital miseries to me by telling me how much her husband loved sports. She went on to tell me how it monopolized his time and how she felt neglected in the marriage.

Though I would never condone a spouse loving a hobby to the detriment of his or her marriage, the accused was not the one standing in front of me. Therefore, if my advice had any chance of taking hold, I thought I had better give this lady something that she could personally do to promote change. I remember going away impressed with my counsel, but I am not so sure she shared in my sentiment.

After listening semi-intently while trying to enjoy my food, I asked this woman how long her husband had a love affair with sports. As she rolled her eyes, she said with a sigh, "Ever since I have known him."

My next question was, "How did you handle this issue before marriage?"

The woman's response was intriguing. Sheepishly, she began by saying that before marriage she pretended that she liked sports, and, whenever he was watching a sporting event, she was right there with him cheering on his team. The enthusiasm in the conversation started to change as I asked her why she ever stopped. She had to admit that she had only played along before marriage because she liked him and she wanted to win him over.

If my memory serves me correct, my advice to this bewildered woman was simple, biblical, yet not well received. I encouraged her to grab a sports jersey and return to her first works. Unfortunately, the conversation was short lived as she seemed to be unwilling to give in the relationship without a guarantee of receiving from her husband.

In Luke 6:38, Jesus taught:

> *"Give, and it shall be given unto you; good measure, pressed down, and shaken together, and running over, shall men give into your bosom. For with the same measure that ye mete withal it shall be measured to you again."*

Normally, teachers make an application to money after quoting this verse. Honestly, if you read this verse in its proper context, it has very little to do with money and more to do with offering kindness and forgiveness to others. Jesus is teaching that if you want kindness from others, you must first learn to give it away.

In a marital situation, if you desire the other person to stretch to meet your needs, you will first have to be willing to be stretched. If you expect the other to take interest in you, you may have to take the plunge and show interest in what they love before they are willing to return the favor. Any other type of approach will leave your marriage at what I call a stalemate, with both deeply entrenched in their pride and skepticism.

From a very practical perspective, this means not to walk six feet behind your wife while she is shopping, while you shuffle your feet in silent protest of the entire shopping experience. It means even though you do not understand your husband's fascination with engines, his lawnmower, fishing, or sports, you work hard at not taking those subtle little verbal jabs at his obsessions.

Keep in mind, different is not weird, strange, or wrong. It is just different.

I do not understand many of the conversations or desires that my wife has concerning clothing, home decor, make up, or hair. Honestly, at times, I think that women have their own separate language concerning some of these items, as I often hear words that seem new to the English language. But, if I roll my eyes, sigh, or even start to make little sarcastic jokes about the things she holds dear to her heart, how can I ever expect her to show patience and especially interest toward mine? Truly, it is more blessed to give than to receive, and it is only when we give in these areas that we should we ever expect to receive anything back from our spouse.

It is in the Bible

Paul, in I Corinthians 13:5, shares something very remarkable about charity or true love. Under Divine Influence, Paul said:

> "[Charity] Doth not behave itself unseemly, seeketh
> not her own, is not easily provoked, thinketh no evil;"

I often use I Corinthians 13:5 when advising couples, in that it shows us that love is not about our personal bent, likes, nor dislikes. Love is identifying the needs and desires of another person and striving to meet those needs regardless of our disposition. This is why the verse states that charity or biblical love "seeketh not her own."

I sometimes hear people convey in almost a defiant manner that they are not into the personal interests of their spouse. When I attempt to encourage these very same people to move contrary to what comes natural to them, they often come back with statements as such:

"That's just not my personality."

"I can't act like a robot."

"I just can't be fake."

"It is important for me to be me."

"I think love should come more naturally than that."

First off, whenever I hear these statements, it is usually the sign of someone with an unwilling heart to submit to biblical precepts. Their retorts are not typically a sign of a lack of understanding as much as a lack of willingness to love unconditionally.

Secondly, it should be noted that God has never asked you to do that which comes natural concerning your spouse, as much as He desires for you to abide under the influence of the Supernatural. According to the Word, He exhorts us to love others with a love that is derived from above. Notice how this thought is conveyed in Romans 5:5:

*"And hope maketh not ashamed; because the love of
God is shed abroad in our hearts by the Holy Ghost
which is given unto us."*

Romans 5:5 teaches us that the "love of God" is in the heart of every believer. This is key in that every child of God has the ability to love in the same way that God, Himself, would love. This, my friend, is a very powerful love that provides us the ability to love in a way that our natural man is not able. In my estimation, I would much rather love in this manner, as there is no greater love than the love that God, Himself, has to offer.

Thirdly, I have already alluded to the fact that my wife has wants and desires that seldom incite warm fuzzies inside of me. However, if my understanding is correct, love is not about the giver as much as it is about the receiver, and my joy as a husband and a father primarily comes from seeing them full of joy and happiness.

Romans 12:15 commands Christians to "rejoice with them that do rejoice." There is much to be learned from this verse in that joy and happiness are not simply found in getting what we want in life. Real joy comes from finding joy in the fact that others are finding their way. (Acts 20:35)

The principle that we may extract from Romans 12:15 is not simply sage advice or a great marriage tip. It is what adults do, and, for some of us, we will do well to grow up and stop basing our happiness on the service that others can provide for us, but rather our service toward them.

Thought-Provoking Questions:

1. The second step of our 2-step process is to study your spouse and act accordingly, but it is broken down into two distinct parts. What are the two parts of the second step?

2. What are a few of the reasons as to why opposites attract?

3. Are there traits that attracted you to your spouse that caused you to repel from one another at a later time? Can you provide a few examples?

4. What are some differences between you and your spouse?

5. What is the snow versus the cold concerning these differences? That is, how do the differences between you and your spouse help you, and how do you perceive that they hinder you at times?

6. Have you been focused on the cold for so long, that you have stopped acknowledging and appreciating the differences between you and your spouse?

7. Does your spouse have interests that seem nonsensical to you?

8. Is love about you, or the needs and desires of your spouse? (I Corinthians 13:5)

9. Are we to love our spouse as long as it comes naturally, or are we to display a supernatural love? (Romans 5:5)

10. How can you better take interest in the interests of your spouse?

Closing Prayer:

*Lord, move us outside of ourselves
and into the interests of our spouse.
Give us a love for them that can
only be explained by the Supernatural.*

Chapter 11

SAFETY FENCE

Ihave had the pleasure of meeting a few couples that have been married for over sixty years. One such couple was in my last pastorate. Their names were Walt and Alice.

Many Sundays, you could hear Alice calling for her husband across the auditorium by saying, "Lover! Are you ready to go home?" On another occasion, as they were making their way to their car, I overheard her saying, "What a beautiful night! It's a night for lovers!"

I remember once asking Walt the key to their success as a married couple. He thought for a few moments and said, "Years ago, my wife told me that if I was to ever leave her, everything would be split in two. She would get the inside and I would get the outside." He added, "So, I thought I had just as well stay with her. "

During my tenure as pastor at that church, I watched Walt and Alice very closely as I often marveled at the love they shared. Though God had obviously blessed them for their faithfulness to Him and their love for His Word, I noticed something else that few seem to possess: even though they were in their mid eighties, they felt comfortable acting like little children around each other.

I have a few definitions of what makes a great marriage. This is probably my favorite:

A great marriage is when two full grown adults feel safe and vulnerable enough to allow the little children within themselves to come out of their respective houses and talk and play with one another.

If you think about it, when your relationship with your spouse is at peak performance, you feel like acting like little children around each other. When you feel the most in love with your mate, you exhibit a playful spirit toward one another. Quite simply, you are like two little children laughing and playing on the playground of vulnerability.

Every one of us are little children deep down inside. Even the scriptures refer to adult believers in Christ as "little children" in I John 2:1.

Have you ever been to a bridal or a baby shower and witnessed the behavior of the ladies? As they laugh, talk, and play their little games, you would think that they were all ten years old again.

If you are ever around a group of men when they are relaxed and feeling free from the pressures of life, what do you find? Grown men acting like little boys again.

For Melody and I, our greatest moments as a married couple are not marked by money spent or assets acquired. Our high times are measured by the same standard that was present just a few months upon meeting: we both feel free to talk, run, play, and even fall to the ground on that playground of safety and vulnerability.

Life sometimes requires us to have a tough exterior. It is true that in certain situations and environments it would be unwise to reveal your thoughts or your feelings. (Matthew 7:6) A home, on the other hand, is to be a different setting. In a biblical home, all involved should be able to dream, verbalize their dreams, trip up over themselves, laugh, and even cry without feeling ridiculed or demeaned. Sad to say, this type of an atmosphere seems to be a rarity in even many so-called Christian homes.

If marriage is ever to be enjoyed as God intends, then both participants will have to find a way to encourage the other to step out of their carefully guarded house and into a place of safety. In the next few pages, we will learn how to promote an atmosphere of safety in a marriage even in the face of conflict.

Tricky Part of Marriage

The tricky part of marriage is having the wisdom to act enough like adults so that both feel safe enough to act like little children around each other. In order to accomplish this, I have found it essential to encourage couples to set up what I call a safety fence in their relationship.

Many seem to view the word "conflict" as if it is a curse word or something to be associated with yelling, screaming, and hurt feelings. If this is your perception of the word, then some rethinking may be in order. (Romans 12:2)

Many are from homes where if there was a disagreement then unhealthy conflict was the order, or should I restate, the disorder of the day. Disagreements equaled hurt feelings. Not seeing eye to eye meant that someone may finally get their way, but only at another's expense. One may win, but only after someone else suffered a loss.

It seems that for many, conflict has seldom served as a bridge to a deeper intimacy with others, but rather a cliff, over which their relationships have tragically fallen.

Like a knife, conflict can be used for our betterment or our detriment. We can take hold of it by the blade or by the handle.

My wife and I are not close today because everything has been perfect. We have unity because the heat of conflict has melted our hearts together in almost an inseparable union that was not present the first few years of marriage.

Conflict is not a dirty word. Even the scriptures bear this out:

"He that rebuketh a man afterwards shall find more favour than he that flattereth with the tongue."
(Proverb 28:23)

"Open rebuke is better than secret love."
(Proverbs 27:5)

"Moreover if thy brother shall trespass against thee, go and tell him his fault between thee and him alone: if he shall hear thee, thou hast gained thy brother."
(Matthew 18:15)

As you can see, the scriptures are showing us that good can arise from conflict. However, it must be noted that unless couples stay in what I call a safety fence, they will see but few blessings flowing from it. In reality, they will waste away those opportunities to walk over the bridge of conflict that leads to a more intimate fellowship with one another. Instead, they will find themselves falling once again off the edge of the cliff of unhealthy conflict, all the while blaming each other for the tragic fall.

The Planks of the Safety Fence

As previously mentioned, a great marriage is when two people feel safe and vulnerable enough to come out of their tough exterior and talk and play with one another like little children. When this is not occurring in a marriage, in a figurative sense, one of three scenarios are often in play:

1. Both the husband and the wife end up fighting on their respective playground. Wherefore, what is designed to be a playground of vulnerability morphs into a battleground where both feel a need to stand in a defensive posture.

2. One runs inside their house and locks the door while the other chases after them. It is not long before the one chasing is banging on the door and pleading for the other to come out.

3. One runs inside and locks the door, yet they are upset because the other is not chasing after them.

Either way, the three paradigms mentioned are not so much the result of the presence of conflict, as they are an inability to handle conflict in a biblical fashion.

When conflict comes, I greatly encourage couples to stay in the safety fence. That is, I exhort them to agree to disagree by staying within biblical boundary lines. The planks that make up this safety fence are these:

No Yelling

Though you may think otherwise, your spouse is not deaf. Therefore, there is no need to raise the decibels on your volume.

With some couples, there may be words constantly exchanged as such:

Spouse #1: "Stop yelling!"

Spouse #2: "I'm not yelling."

Spouse #1: "It sounds like yelling to me."

If the previous exchange is fairly common in your conversations, then a good rule of thumb is that, in relationships, perception is reality. That is, it is not what you think that you are doing that matters, as much as what the other person is perceiving you are doing that should be the primary concern. In other words, though you may not feel that you are raising your voice, if the other person perceives it as yelling, then you should focus on speaking in a more gentle fashion.

I do understand that there are a few exceptions to this rule in that some filter even normal conversation through the pain of their past. Be that as it may, it is still best to follow the previously mentioned rule of thumb to the best of your ability.

No Physical Contact

This plank would involve any type of grabbing, hitting, blocking, confining, or slapping, and it applies to the woman as well as the man.

No Name Calling or Cursing

Couples should refrain from using words and phrases that are demeaning to the other person's self esteem. Ephesians 4:29 speaks to this matter as it instructs us:

> *"Let no corrupt communication proceed out of your*
> *mouth, but that which is good to the use of edifying,*
> *that it may minister grace unto the hearers."*

The word "edifying" has its roots in the same word used for edifice which refers to a building. Through Ephesians 4:29, the Lord is encouraging us to use words that build up those around us. Obviously, words such as stupid, jerk, and idiot will do little to cause us to walk in alignment with this verse of scripture.

As far as cursing is concerned, it should be understood that a curse word is simply the peak of a mountain of unbelief and anger. A person that has to revert to using curse words is exclaiming their lack of faith in God and their inability to solve the issue in a more refined manner.

Also, I would encourage those of a more religious nature to refrain from spiritualizing or Christianizing their name calling by using phrases such as these:

"You're rebellious."

"You are acting like a reprobate."

"You just seem so hard-hearted."

"I think you are an un-submissive wife."

"Your are full of the devil."

"You need the Holy Ghost."

"You should get right with God."

Whereas one may be right in their assessment of their spouse, he or she will usually find that they will wrong their relationship by using such phrases in the heat of a moment.

Stick with the Facts

When couples fight, they often resort to making broad, general statements like, "You do that all the time," or, "You say this every time," or, "This always happens," or, "You never do that."

While there may be consistency to the negative behavior of your spouse, I usually find that these statements are not entirely true. This is problematic for two basic reasons:

1. Couples that make such statements are usually walking contrary to Philippians 4:8 and Ephesians 4:15.

Philippians 4:8 commands us to focus on things that are one hundred percent truthful. Whereas there may be an element of truth to the statements listed above, it should be noted that ninety-nine percent truth is still one hundred percent error.

2. I find that such words and phrases are extremely demoralizing for a spouse that is trying to better themselves.

Oftentimes, a struggling spouse will be on their best behavior for two or three days and then revert to a few old habits. If they are met with words such as, "You always do that," or, "I am so tired of you doing this all the time," they will feel discouraged about the advances they previously made for the better.

Stick with the Present

It is perfectly fine to consider the past, as long as both are in a problem solving mode. But, if you or your spouse are using the past just to lash out, get even, or win the argument, it should be considered off limits.

Do not Argue Around the Children

One of the greatest assets parents have when it comes to providing a healthy environment for their children is unity and joy in the marriage. If these do not exist, the hearts and minds of their children are exposed to what I call the elements of pain and heartache, long before they have the capacity to handle such emotions.

Unity and joy between a husband and a wife serve as a bridge upon which their children safely walk. When this bridge is collapsing, fear, anguish, and insecurity will fill their hearts, and, unfortunately, negative repercussions always follow.

You may have moments where you and your spouse disagree, but, for the most part, your children need to see a united front. Take your conversations to another room or schedule them at a different time.

Do not Argue Late into the Night

Late at night, when they are tired, people feel deeper and say things out of character. Hence, I find that engaging in serious discussion after 10:30 pm is disastrous for many couples.

In response to this plank, some have asked me about the verse in Ephesians 4:26 that says, ". . . let not the sun go down upon your wrath." My answer to this is quite simple: if you are having to break five other commands to keep this one command, then maybe you should give up on the fight and go to bed.

Have you ever found yourself extremely concerned about a matter until the wee hours of the morning only to wake up the next day and the worries seem smaller? Early in marriage, this was commonplace for me, and one of the greatest lessons that I learned was that a good night's sleep is therapeutic to the soul.

As a pastor, I sometimes receive late night calls from people that are in the middle of a marital altercation. I often give them extremely simple advice: Go to bed and see if you even care about the issue in the morning. I rarely hear from those couples the next day, as sleep has a way of shining a light on what can appear very dark and gruesome in the night.

Watch Your Tone of Voice

It has been said that ninety percent of communication is non-verbal. That being the case, we must be careful to watch not only what we are saying, but how we are saying it.

Couples often have a way of speaking one thing with their words yet another with their tone of voice. This often happens by making remarks like, "Why were you late?" or, "Where did you go after work?" in a very heated manner.

In cases as such, an honest question is asked with their words, yet a harsh statement is made with their tone of voice. Though their words ask a question, their tone of voice communicates that they have already tried, convicted, and sentenced the accused before having an ample hearing. This is always a mistake in that a spouse is not asking a question as much as conveying their anger and their frustration under the guise of a question.

Proverbs speaks to this matter as it states:

"He that answereth a matter before he heareth it, it is folly and shame unto him." (Proverbs 18:13)

Emotionally, many spouses come to conclusions before they have heard all of the facts. Ergo, when they speak, their tone of voice is contradicting their seemingly interested or caring words, and the conversation ends in a downward spiral.

No Interrupting

Quite simply, it is disrespectful to interrupt the other person's talk. Of course, this does not give one license to monopolize a conversation for thirty minutes at a time, but an adherence to this principle will help conversations to stay at deescalated levels.

No Sarcasm

Sarcasm it simply a subtle way to vent our frustrations and our anger. Though it is probably okay to use sarcasm toward politicians, it is off limits in a family scenario.

We have a rule in our house that has helped us to stay on track over the years: if someone in our home is not having fun, then nobody should be having fun.

Keep in mind that a home is to be a safe atmosphere where all involved should be able to come out of their tough exterior and feel safe to express themselves in a godly manner. Unfortunately, in many homes, sarcasm causes many of the family members to be in a state of emotional survival rather than safety. Honestly, no matter how Christian these homes purport to be, it is utter ungodliness. (I John 4:8)

Do Not Bully Through Questions

Some spouses ask questions during a discussion, but they are not happy with the answers. When this occurs, they continue by asking the same question over and over again. In my view, this is not healthy communication, as a real question is not being asked. The interrogator is actually bullying through questioning.

If you are going to ask a real question, then I would encourage you to accept the answer, even if it fails to meet your expectations. If the other is lying to you, time will tell, as that which is hidden has a way of eventually being revealed. (Luke 12:2)

Table the Matter

In spite of seeing a number of counselors, some couples still struggle to find their footing. Here are two predominant reasons as to why I feel couples in such a state fail to make forward progress:

1. Either one or both parties are unwilling to give it their all unless they have an absolute guarantee that everything will turn out for the better.

2. Some couples become so caught up in their emotions that they seem to be unable to table a matter until they are in a better emotional state.

One of the keys to effective communication in a marriage is learning how and when to talk about an issue. If couples only talk about matters when emotions are high, they will seldom find good results.

If a conversation is emotionally charged, I highly recommend tabling the issue for a later time. If not, you will find it difficult to stay within the planks of the recommended safety fence.

Here are a few steps that should help you to implement the very important practice of tabling a discussion until a later time:

Step #1 - It is vital to learn to sense when your spouse's spirit is starting to close and a wall of emotion is being erected between the both of you. An inability to discern such a state will cause a multitude of issues in your marriage.

Step #2 - Agree to table the subject at hand until a later time, before your playground turns into a battleground. This waiting period should serve to allow time to erode that wall of emotion and give both of you ample time to serve one another.

Step #3 - During the waiting period, be sure to serve one another so as to open the spirit of the other person. As mentioned in chapter four, until the spirit of your spouse is open, you will fail to gain access to their intellect. If you reverse this order, you will fail at conveying your thoughts in an effective manner, and you will continue the saga of walking away and accusing the other of being unreasonable.

Step #4 - If you table an item, be sure to revisit the item as agreed. Do not take for granted that all is settled because there is peace in the house. Live up to your word and deal with the matter, all the while staying within a biblical safety fence.

Step #5 - Leave a caveat to step four in that it is entirely permissible to forgo revisiting certain items as long as both of you are in agreement. This is due to the fact that many couples fight over matters that they will care little about in just a few short hours.

Thought-Provoking Questions:

1. A great marriage is when two people feel safe and vulnerable enough to come out of their tough exterior and talk and play with one another like little children. Is there an atmosphere of safety and vulnerability in your marriage, especially in conversation?

2. Would your spouse agree with your answer?

3. When a fight occurs in your marriage, what happens? Do both of you engage in battle, or does one person end up shutting themselves inside their respective house, while the other lingers outside?

4. Has conflict in your marriage ever yielded beneficial results?

5. Does all conflict in marriage have to yield negative results? (Proverbs 28:23, Proverbs 27:5, and Matthew 18:15)

6. Have you and your spouse taken the knife of conflict by the blade or by the handle? That is, has it been used to forge a better relationship, or one that is worse?

7. Which planks of the safety fence are you and your spouse tempted to jump?

8. Has your marriage ever benefited from jumping outside of the prescribed safety zone?

9. What are some things that you can do to make your spouse feel safe in the relationship?

10. Are you and your spouse good about tabling a matter until a later time?

11. Do you see the benefit of tabling a matter as long as both agree to revisit it at an appointed time?

Closing Prayer:

Lord, help us as husbands and wives
to move our marriages to a higher level.
Give us grace to replace selfish behavior
with biblical behavior.

Chapter 12

CLOSING THOUGHTS

Raise the Floor

Most of us know that we should set high goals and raise the standard for excellence in our marriages. However, have you ever considered that instead of raising the ceiling, you may need to raise the floor?

Once again, most couples understand the need for reaching new heights, but many have not considered adjusting the standard on how low they will go in an argument or a heated discussion.

For some couples, words relating to divorce and separation easily flow from their mouths while in the midst of an argument. This occurs when using expressions like: "I hate you," or, "I should have never married you," or, "I'm leaving," or, "I want a divorce."

If this is a common occurrence in your marriage, instead of raising the bar, you may need to find a landing cushion a little higher off of the ground. That is, it will serve you well to agree to rid your marriage of such expressions that not only cut to the heart, but are utterly hateful in intent.

If your marriage has suffered from this kind of talk, I would encourage you to apologize to one another and agree to disagree in a much more refined fashion.

Even the worst of enemies over the years have given some type of pittance toward rules of war. If opposing factions of hostile nations can abide by such rules, then maybe spouses should do the same.

A Jewel from Matthew Henry

Matthew Henry said it well when he said:

> "He that has a good God, a good heart, and a good wife, to converse with, and yet complains . . . would not have been easy and content in paradise;"[6]

If a man has a good relationship with God and a pleasant fellowship with his family, what more is there to have? If we need more than these, then, as Mr. Henry shows us, we would not have been happy in God's garden.

As a happily married man with beautiful children and the hope of Heaven, there is nothing I will receive tomorrow that will make me happier than I am today. That being the case, then these areas are where my priorities should lie.

Thought-Provoking Questions:

1. Do you easily exchange words and phrases that are unfair and cut to the heart?

2. Have the words, "I hate you," or "I want a divorce," ever helped your relationship?

3. Do you see a need to raise the floor in your marriage?

4. If you filtered everything you said to your spouse through Ephesians 4:29, would your conversations with your spouse be different?

5. Outside of your relationship with Christ, is your marriage your number one priority in life?

6. If paradise for Adam and Eve was a perfect relationship with God and one another, then should these not be our primary pursuits in life?

A Closing Prayer

Lord, for those that have not the Spirit of Christ,
I pray that through faith in the Name of Jesus they would
receive Your grace. Also, for those that have lost
but all hope in their marriage, give them the grace
to persevere and continue fighting for their marriage
in a way that pleases You as well as their spouse.

To order our Audio Series on marriage,
*How to Fight for Your Marriage
Without Fighting with One Another,*
in CD or MP3 format,
check out our resource page at
www.Shop.HittingHomeMinistry.com

END NOTES:

1. Dr. Adrian Rogers, May 09, 2009. "Devotionals by Love Worth Finding", Love Worth Finding, Retreived from http://www.oneplace.com/ministries/love-worth-finding/read/devotionals/love-worth-finding/love-worth-finding-may-9-11603374-11603374.html.

2. Jon Ware, July 10, 2009. "Yes, family breakdown is behind broken Britain.", Mail Online, Retrieved from http://www.dailymail.co.uk/debate/article-1198962/Yes-family-breakdown-IS-broken-Britain-Top-judge-says-national-tragedy-attacks-BBC-suppressing-debate.html.

3. Michael Pearl, No Greater Joy, "Joy of the Parents," Pleasantville, TN: No Greater Joy Ministries, Inc., 1997, p. 2.

4. Linda J. Waite, Don Browning, William J. Doherty, Maggie Gallagher, Ye Luo, and Scott M. Stanley, Does Divorce Make People Happy, New York, NY: Institue for American Values, p. 12.

5. Matthew Henry, Matthew Henry Commentary, Iowa Falls, IA: World Wide Publishers, Volume 1, p. 274.

6. Matthew Henry, Matthew Henry Commentary, Iowa Falls, IA: World Wide Publishers, Volume 1, p. 19.